THE ECONOMIC EMANCIPATION
OF
AFRICAN-AMERICANS

"Let The Church Say, Amen!!"

by

Richard E. Barber, Sr.

D1320112

PENNY POWER • PENNY POWER • PENNY POWER

THE ECONOMIC EMANCIPATION
OF
AFRICAN-AMERICANS

"Let The Church Say, Amen!!"

Copyright © 1990 By Richard E. Barber, Sr.

Printed in the United States of America

All rights reserved. No part of this publication may be reproduced, stored in a retrieval system, or transmitted in any form or by any means, electronic, mechanical, photo-copying, recording, otherwise, without the prior permission in writing from the Author, except for brief quotations included in a review of the book. Address inquiries to Penny Lovers of America Inc., P.O. Box 6141, Somerset, New Jersey 08875-6141.

Copies of this book are available at $7.95 per copy plus $2.00 for postage and handling from:

Penny Lovers of America, Inc.
P.O. Box 6141
Somerset, New Jersey 08875-6141

Library of Congress
Catalog Card Number   91-060157

PENNY POWER • PENNY POWER • PENNY POWER

THE ECONOMIC EMANCIPATION OF AFRICAN-AMERICANS

"Let The Church Say, Amen!!"

Richard E. Barber Sr.

Published By

Penny Lovers of America, Inc.
P.O. Box 6141
Somerset, New Jersey 08875-6141

PENNY POWER • PENNY POWER • PENNY POWER

DEDICATION

To my loving wife Betty, and to our children, Vicky, Ricky and Sha-Sha, whose sacrifices and support enabled me to, in the words of the Scriptures as found in Habakkuk 2:2, "Write the vision and make it plain," I shall forever be grateful.

TABLE OF CONTENTS

Page

At the banquet table of nature there are no reserved seats. You get what you can take, and keep what you can hold. If you can't take anything, you won't get anything; and if you can't hold anything, you won't keep anything. And you can't take anything without organization.

- A. Philip Randolph

GET UP AND DO!

You sit and quarrel all your life,
And blame the moving world at large:
You fail to enter the strife,
To sail in fortune's happy barge.

Get up my man and do the 'stuff'
That leads the blazing glory's fame:
Hold on, and be like good Macduff,
And damn the man who'd foil you' name.

--Marcus Garvey

FOREWORD

The Black church has been the center of the Black community since its inception in the closing decade of the eighteenth century. The church provided the leadership, the schools and the spiritual and moral support for persons who were destined to remain marginal in America for another two hundred years.

One problem always remained unresolved, however; that was the formation of capital for the financing of Black enterprises in business and industry. Small efforts were abundant and successful, but apart from Maggie Walker's beauty products and the insurance companies there was little else to show. We had handsome mortuaries, independent carpenters and masons, blacksmiths, barbers, caterers and draymen, but the big enterprises eluded us.

So, here we are with the churches , strong and well staffed and supported on the one hand, and on the other hand, a huge vacuum in business enterprises.

Richard Barber is a creative and industrious person. In Pittsburgh a new Black bank sprang into being under his guidance and direction. He is haunted by the dream of capital formation among Blacks, the churches primarily, looking forward to a serious change in the face of the Black communities in America.

With modest success this point could be made convincing, and momentum could grow and give this dream reality. Everything has a beginning with an idea, and Dick Barber's idea may be a true beginning.

Samuel D. Proctor
Pastor Emeritus
Abyssinian Baptist
Church and Professor
Emeritus, Martin Luther
King Jr. Chair
Rutgers University

PREFACE

One of the key concerns of most African-Americans is the conservative mood of the nation which has resulted in an increasing climate of hostility and insensitivity to our hopes, dreams, and aspirations as a people. Let us remember, however, that our struggle for survival and full citizenship in a hostile environment is nothing new. Our history is replete with example after example of our struggle against racism, discrimination and injustice. Yet, our faith, determination and hope have kept us going toward a brighter day and full participation in the American experiment.

Once again we are witnessing sinister forces challenging our institutions and our progress. These forces are causing much suffering and hardship in our communities, especially among the poor and the elderly. In response to these forces, we hear voices from the past pleading with us to unite, organize and take responsibility for our destiny. The voice of Booker T. Washington says, "Cast down your buckets where you are; develop your resources and talents for self-sufficiency." We hear the voice of Dr. Mary McLeod Bethune echoing the legacy she left us. We hear the thunderous voice of Frederick Douglass saying, " where there is no struggle, there is no progress.

Power concedes nothing without a demand, it never has and never will." The eloquent voice of Dr. Martin Luther King, Jr. calls upon us, "to straighten our backs because no one can ride your back unless it is bent."

Friends, we are indeed facing difficult and trying times. These times do not demand "summer soldiers nor sunshine patriots." These times require dedicated and firmly committed persons to the cause of 'economic emancipation' and meaningful progress. We need an army of volunteers who, day in and day out, week after week, month after month, will work untiringly and unselfishly on an agenda of progress on many fronts, facing possible obstacles and disappointments with a determined resolve.

I am grateful to those volunteers who have heard the voices out of the past of our fallen heroes and heeded their pleading. May we continue to work together diligently to improve the quality of life in our communities by solving some of the problems and difficult situations our people face on a daily basis. May we "walk together little children and don't get weary" on this historic journey toward Economic Emancipation. Remember:

"IF YOU ARE NOT PART OF THE SOLUTION, THEN YOU ARE PART OF THE PROBLEM."

INTRODUCTION AND ACKNOWLEDGEMENTS

I do not know how much longer I have to live on this earth. In fact, none of us do. Consequently, I feel an impelling personal sense of urgency that time is running out for me and my fellow African-Americans to create a sound economic foundation on which future generations can build. My mission now is simply to do God's will and fulfill 'the vision' which He has given me by implementing the <u>Economic Emancipation Plan for African-Americans</u>. This "God-given vision" has engulfed my life and like Jeremiah "it's like fire, shut up in my bones." I only pray that my notes, personal records, and my memory reflect the depth and intensity of that fire and I can accurately convey this message to African-Americans and especially my generation. I write this message out of deep concern for the economic conditions of African-Americans. I write this message under the inspiration of God, fully aware that the words and thoughts which shall flow from the depths of my heart and the reservoir of my mind are the result of the creativity and unlimited wisdom of God. I am only an instrument--a vessel--used by God to convey this message to a confused, downtrodden and seemingly a hopeless people still wandering in the wilderness 127 years after the Emancipation Proclamation--that their present conditions and circumstances in no ways reflect his power and goodness.

For years now I have quietly observed the sad state of affairs of Black America while leaving to others the task of providing a larger vision for our people and a meaningful 'self-help' initiative to match that larger vision. This period of reflection and introspection has revealed the pains of poverty and wide-spread human suffering, a sense of hopelessness and economic dependency of a great and noble people. The state of Black America reminds me of the Book of Nehemiah in the Bible and the challenges Nehemiah faced in rebuilding the gates, the walls, and the City of Jerusalem. I have been admonished by the words of Dr. Howard Thurman who wrote, "Those who are able to speak the truth and don't speak it, then anybody may speak."

I cannot hold my peace any longer for my own life has been touched and enriched by some giants of our race and I must now share that "torch of knowledge and fountain of blessings" with others.

God gave me loving, wonderful, caring and Christian parents, who nurtured me in a Christian home. Their personal commitment to God and to educational enrichment provided me a set of values which have served me well, and gave me a deep, unbridled thirst for education and learning which grows stronger as the years unfold.

I was blessed to have had some "caring and sensitive" teachers in that "separate but equal school" down in Jones County, North Carolina, during my formative years. From Mr. C.C. Franks, my elementary, junior high and high school principal to my teachers-- Mrs. Gladys Brown, Mrs. Leah Franks, Miss Hazel Mallette, Mrs. Mazie Isler, Miss Sudie Mabel Dockery, Mrs. Virginia McDaniel Payton, Rev. Robert F. Johnson, Mrs. Mary O. Davis, Mr. J. I. Barber, Mrs. O. K. Grady, Mrs. Ida Smith Franks, Miss Vassy Ward, Mr. Aaron Green, Mr. Arlin S. Bryant, Mrs. J. W. Willie, Mr David O'Pharrow, Miss Dorothy Hart, Mr. D. W. Murrell, Mr. James Wynn, Mr. C. A. Jordan and Mr. Fletcher Barber, my 4-H Club leader-- even with 'hand-me-down' books and limited educational equipment and supplies, they all went the extra miles to ensure maximum education and learning opportunities.

I was blessed to attend North Carolina A&T College (now North Carolina A&T State University) where instructors and professors touched my mind and soul, and gave this 'little old country boy' a larger vision of himself and the world.

I have been richly blessed to have had some giants of our race as role models and heroes, and their tutelage and friendship have made them VSP (Very Special People) in my life. The late Mr. C.C. Franks, my principal, Dr. Warmouth T. Gibbs, Dr. Samuel D. Proctor, and

Dr. Lewis C. Dowdy, Presidents of North Carolina A&T during my studies there in 1958-1962. Dr. Proctor has remained a personal advisor, friend and hero even until this day, twenty-nine (29) years later.

Dr. Donald Edwards, my college physics professor and advisor at A&T, and a 'father figure' to his students; Dr. Leon Sullivan whose philosophy influenced me to give up a promising corporate career in 1969 and join O.I.C (Opportunities Industrialization Center) in Pittsburgh.

Actor Ossie Davis, whose great speech at the first Congressional Black Caucus Dinner in Washington, D.C., in June 1971 (It's Not the Man, It's the Plan, It's Not the Rap, It's the Map) had such a tremendous impact on my life. I returned to Pittsburgh and became involved in the founding of a full-service commercial bank--New World National Bank-- and the writing of the Economic Emancipation Plan for African-Americans (1971-1981). In 1985 Mr. Davis recorded on video "A Penny Speaks" which I wrote in 1984 and is the basis for my work with church, business and community groups in improving the economic status of African-Americans. The late Dr. Vivian Henderson, President of Clark College and an economist, who in 1971 took time from his busy schedule to meet with Al Smith (now President of South Carolina State) and me in Atlanta to review and critique the College and

University Endowment (CUE) component of the <u>Economic Emancipation Plan</u> and to offer suggestions and encouragement. Reverend Isaac Green, my pastor and spiritual advisor and those inspirational 'kitchen chats' over tea cakes and milk in his home during a very turbulent and trying period in my life, the founding and organizing of New World National Bank.

The late Dr. Brannon J. Hopson, a minister and a personal friend whose leadership in the Pittsburgh church community resulted in over 200 churches supporting the organizing efforts of New World National Bank and providing the necessary initial capital. I cannot mention the organizing efforts of New World National Bank without paying special tribute to Jim Lewis, Mrs. Willa Mae Rice and the late Mrs. Hazel Garland of the <u>New</u> <u>Pittsburgh</u> <u>Courier</u> for their extraordinary efforts and contributions in promoting New World National Bank, "an idea whose time had come."

Dr. Benjamin L.Hooks, who gave me the opportunity to serve as Deputy Executive Director of the National NAACP with that giant Mr. Clarence Mitchell, Jr. and view America, and especially Black America, from a very key and strategic vantage point. This was a very rewarding and educational experience.

In short, as that old spiritual goes, "Lord, I'm Blessed," and I shall be eternally grateful to those persons named and scores of others unnamed who have played such a key part in my personal development and earned a very special place in my life. To all who know me or get to know me, I must humbly say, "Be patient with me, God is not through with me yet."

Now I must share the experience and the 'vision' which God has revealed to me by conveying a <u>Message</u> and <u>Plan</u> of <u>Economic Emancipation</u> to my fellow African-Americans. I do so with the hope that they will support this mission to lift the economic standards of our people so that they too may truly participate in the "American Dream."

I am especially indebted to Dr. Chancellor Williams whose book, <u>The Destruction of Black Civilization,</u> provided additional "fire in my belly" and a renewed commitment to continue this Economic Emancipation journey and hopefully right some of the economic wrongs of history. Our long distance telephone conversations, and a meeting and interview with him to discuss his book have given me renewed inspiration and a greater sense of mission to follow my dreams and implement this 'vision.'

I am deeply indebted to Bishop Frank C. Cummings of Philadelphia for accepting the Chairmanship of the Economic Emancipation Advisory Board and the Board of Advisors for their wise counsel, guidance and direction to our cause and efforts.

My gratitude also goes to Mel Blount, former Pittsburgh Steeler for his leadership of our Annual National Penny Campaign sponsored by Penny Lovers of America, Inc., and to the scores of professional athletes and entertainers who have committed themselves to this cause of Economic Emancipation of African-Americans.

Finally, we read in the Bible that God gave Moses a 'rod' and he led Children of Israel out of Egypt and years of bondage to the Promised Land.

God gave Dr. George Washington Carver the "humble peanut and sweet potato" and he revolutionized and revitalized the South with hundreds of products which created thousands of jobs in a dying cotton economy.

I deeply believe that God gave me this "vision of the Penny" and with pennies united we can deliver African-Americans from "Economic Slavery" and on the road toward "Economic Emancipation." The message conveyed by a penny in A Penny Speaks sets the tone and purpose of our journey.

A COMPASS OF OUR OWN

As a young boy growing up on the farm down in North Carolina, I was very active in the 4-H Club--where I served as State President during my junior year in high school--and Boy Scout Troop #204 in Trenton, North Carolina, where I earned my Eagle Scout Award at age 16. During my scouting years, my Scoutmaster, Mr. Dewey Strayhorn, and Explorer Post Advisor, Mr. Aaron Green, would instruct us to always carry a compass on hiking and camping trips. A compass is an instrument which provides one with consistent direction which prevents disorientation and minimizes the possibility of becoming lost. I use to wonder if Biblical history would have been different if Moses would have had a man-made compass during his forty years in the wilderness. However, Bible study later revealed to me that God kept Moses and the Children of Israel in the wilderness for forty years to rid them of that 'slave mentality' and 'we can't' attitudes. God provided Moses a compass in the form of a cloud by day, and a pillar of fire by night. I believe the time is long overdue for African-Americans to develop, with God's help, "A Compass of Our Own" in order to implement an economic agenda and measurable progress for each generation.

Have you ever wondered what it is like as African-Americans and nearly totally dependent on other groups for practically all our goods and services? Visualize this scenario if you will:

"You are awakened in the morning by a clock made by Westinghouse or General Electric, you get from between two sheets made by Cannon Mills; you walk across tile or carpeting from the Armstrong Tile & Cork Company; you go into the bathroom where you turn on a faucet or shower control made by American Standard Company; the water comes down from your local water authority which we don't own nor control; you use soap made by Proctor & Gamble, you step out of the shower and use a Cannon Mills towel to dry your body, you shave using a Gillette or Schick disposable razor; and use Aqua Velva or Old Spice After Shave lotion; you brush your teeth with Close-Up toothpaste and use Scope mouthwash; and use a Faberge Deodorant Stick--and hopefully-Johnson, Soft Sheen, Dudley or Pro-Line Hair Spray. You step into your Hanes underwear, Brooks Brothers suit, Gucci or Florsheim shoes, put on your Stetson hat, pick up your briefcase made by American Leather Company, and walk out to your GM (General Motors) 'Hog' or 'Deuce and a Quarter' in the driveway [for our friends of other persuasions and our uninformed brothers and sisters: a Hog is a Cadillac and a Deuce and a Quarter is a 225 Buick Electra]; you drive off leaving a Toyota Camry made by the Japanese in the driveway for your spouse who is inside hurriedly repeating a similar routine and scenario. You drive off humming 'We Shall Overcome.' And if by chance you meet your fate during the course of the day on 'the man's job,' you are laid to rest in a casket from the National Casket Company, and your flowers come from FTD." How long, oh God, how long?

Have we forgotten the message in that song made famous by the late blues singer Miss Billie Holliday? "Mama may have, and Papa may have, but God bless the child that's got his own."

As wealth in this nation is concentrated in fewer and fewer hands through acquisitions, mergers and the "laying up of treasures by greedy tycoons," we can expect increased poverty, more homelessness, more unemployment, and an increasing number of permanent 'under class' in our communities. As foreign business interests continue to acquire American business enterprises at a rather alarming rate, and American corporate interests continue to seek slave labor markets abroad in their pursuits of greater profits, the overall interests of African-Americans and other minorities of this nation may not be best served. While this situation may present a grim picture, all is not lost. These conditions provide us both a challenge and an opportunity. A challenge to correct some of the past economic wrongs, and an opportunity to develop "<u>A Compass of Our Own</u>."

ECONOMICS AND POLITICS: AN AGENDA OF PROGRESS FOR AFRICAN-AMERICANS

Our generation has a unique opportunity and responsibility to move forward to new horizons and heights through dedication, positive action, and commitment to economic parity and political participation. Those of us who came through the turbulent times of the sixties, whether we were participants, beneficiaries or both, must now consolidate those social gains, and redirect our energies and efforts to a meaningful and measurable economic and political agenda. The time is now that we must implement that agenda and plan for the next generation of African-Americans. It is imperative that we do so with a complete sense of urgency. Let us constantly remind ourselves that "it was not raining when Noah built the ark." Let us, in the words and spirit of Marcus Garvey, "get up and do" and develop what I call the "Bumble Bee philosophy." The Bumble Bee, according to "aeronautical engineers and technical experts," is not supposed to fly. The body is too round and short, the wing span not sufficient for the proper lift forces. Nearly everyone knows all the technical reasons why a Bumble Bee is not supposed to fly, that is, nearly everyone except the Bumble Bee. Therefore, the Bumble Bee just keeps on flying. Let us pay homage to the late A. Philip Randolph by our "organizing efforts and strategies" as we endeavor to claim our rightful place "at the banquet table of nature." His life and work represent the epitome of "organizing genius and commitment to freedom and economic justice."

A short one hundred and twenty-seven (127) years have passed since the shackles of slavery were removed. Since that time, we have seen movements, reorganizations, new programs and some progress, but the real order of things have not changed significantly. Let us be mindful and cognizant of the fact that all movements, reorganizations and new programs do not necessarily represent meaningful progress, for we still find ourselves bound in economic slavery even in 1990.

So often I ask myself just as the slaves did as they were bearing the oppressions, burdens, cruelties and experiencing the long and terrible nightmares of the slave system, "How long, Oh God, how long? How long before we as a people realize and heed the words of our Moses?" Just as in the Biblical days,we have had a Moses in nearly every generation. Remember the thunderous words of Frederick Douglass in 1857 when he stated that "Power concedes nothing without a demand, It never did and it never will. Find out just what people will submit to and you have found out the exact amount of injustice and wrong which may be imposed upon them. And these will continue till they are resisted with either words or blows or both." How proud we must be of the untiring efforts and struggles of Booker T. Washington in establishing Tuskeegee Institute and trying to convince his people to learn a skill or trade for self sufficiency. Have we forgotten the inspiring life and scientific genius of Dr. George Washington Carver; the legacy left us by the great Dr. Mary McLeod Bethune; the foresight of Marcus Garvey pleading with Black Americans to support the development of the African continent in the 1920's. How can we ever forget the eloquent words of Dr. Martin Luther King, Jr., as he spoke of his 'Dream' of a new America, and the courage he demonstrated throughout the South as he pleaded with Black people to 'straighten their backs?'

We have a Moses today in nearly every field of human endeavor. But the sad thing about it is that we never seem to recognize our 'Moses' until their death. Then we jump on the bandwagon, and honor them by naming schools and streets after them; celebrating their birthdays; convening special memorial programs to honor them and awarding plaques and scholarships in their names. In short, we desecrate their life's work by such empty and meaningless gestures. Yet while they lived, usually they were harassed, abused, criticized and isolated. If what they did or said makes sense after their death, why didn't it make sense before their death? "How long Oh God, how long?"

One of the biggest problems we face as a people is the lack of control over our own financial resources. Our insurance premiums, and money which we deposit in banks, savings and loan associations and pension programs provide very little, if any, investment impact in our own communities. It is felt outside our communities, even in places like South Africa with its cruel apartheid system and legal oppression of 28 million Black South Africans, who constitute over eighty percent of its population. Randall Robinson, Executive Director of Trans-Africa, in a speech several years ago, stated that "American banks have over 7 billion dollars in loans in South Africa." The real tragedy of this matter is that a large share of that 7 billion dollars came from African-Americans and, in reality, we, indirectly, are not only subsidizing our own economic and political slavery, but also are helping sustain the slavery and oppression of our brothers and sisters in South Africa. How long, Oh God, how long?

Approximately 95 percent or greater of the money coming into the Black community makes a U-turn and is returned to the general community in a relatively short period of time. I encourage anyone who may doubt the U-turn Theory to test it. One can test this theory by giving himself what I call the <u>Check Test</u>. The next time you pay your bills, itemize them completely and determine how much of the total amount remains in your community and how much it returned to the general community. I contend that approximately ninety-five (95) percent goes back outside the immediate Black community in the form of mortgage and rent payments, food bills, transportation expenses, lottery tickets, entertainment expenses and the like. But the main point is that it goes and usually goes very quickly.

I am led to believe that as African-Americans, we are probably the only ethnic group in the history of this nation who for generation after generation have substantially contributed to the development of nearly everyone else's neighborhood and community except our own. That is a terrible indictment of any ethnic group with a purchasing power of over 300 billion dollars annually. You know, 300 billion dollars "will buy an awful lot of chitterlings."

I am in no way minimizing nor ignoring the traditional and contemporary obstacles which have impeded meaningful economic development in Black communities. But I do believe that if our problems, be they in economics, politics, education, social or housing, are going to be solved, we are going to have to solve them ourselves. We should not realistically expect other people to solve our problems. We must also fully realize that R&R (Rapping and Rhetoric) will not solve our problems. The general community should be called upon for assistance in developing managerial talent and access to capital and markets; but the primary leadership, motivation, and initiative should be our own. Our communities deserve leadership which is bold and courageous, innovative and creative, and willing to endure the risks and penalties of such leadership (See Appendix I).

Finally, those who may question the importance, necessity or practicality of implementing an aggressive economic and political agenda should visit and look around the various Black communities across this nation. A ride through the Hill Districts, Watts, Houghs, Harlems and Bedford-Stuyvesants of America is not a comfortable ride; the beaten faces of beaten men and women aren't happy faces; and a lot of children are still growing up in hand-me-down clothes, living hand-me-down lives. For many people, too long it has been a lip service brotherhood. It's been a bad job, a snow job, or too often it's been no job.

It's been frustration and pessimism and waiting long hours in long lines for hand-outs with a growling stomach. It's been idle hands that could build a skyscraper as easily as cradling a brick; it's been idle minds that could solve complex problems as easily as creating them. Our generation has a unique challenge in order to meet the real needs of our time; a time to crystallize the hopes and dreams of thousands of African-Americans who have lived through urban crises; who have lived where hopes often only mean basic needs and who ask only for an opportunity and a chance to live a decent life.

I encourage and challenge African-Americans and especially the church community of this nation to join and support this noble cause of commitment, vision and accountability in implementing an agenda of progress for our people.

THE ECONOMIC EMANCIPATION PLAN FOR AFRICAN-AMERICANS

"WHERE THERE IS NO VISION, THE PEOPLE PERISH."

Proverbs 29:18

"Thank God for The Vision."

R.E.B.

The philosophy of the Economic Emancipation Plan for African-Americans is embodied in a George Bernard Shaw quotation which was popularized by the late Senator Robert F. Kennedy:

"Some men see things as they are and ask why?...Others have visions and dreams of things that never were and ask why not?"

The inspiration for the development of the Economic Emancipation Plan--which was developed over a ten-year period (1971-1981) came from the Scriptures: "Where there is no vision, the people perish" [Proverbs 29:18]. It serves to the Glory of God for this reason: "Instead of loving money and using people, this program uses money and loves people." Historically, in too many of our churches, the inherent evils of money and wealth have been taught. Namely that, "money is the root of all evil." Yet, in searching the Scriptures for knowledge and teachings on <u>money</u> and <u>wealth</u>, <u>work</u>, <u>savings</u> and <u>giving</u>, we find both support and challenges.

SCRIPTURES TO PONDER (NIV)

MONEY:

"Be careful that you do not forget the Lord your God, failing to observe his commands, his laws and his decrees that I am giving you this day. Otherwise when you eat and are satisfied, when you build fine houses and settle down, and when your herds and flocks grow large and your silver and gold increase and all you have is multiplied, then your heart will become proud and you will forget the Lord your God, who brought you out of Egypt, out of the land of slavery. But remember the Lord your God, for it is he who gives you the ability to produce wealth, and so confirms his covenant, which he swore to your forefathers, as it is today." (Deuteronomy 8:11-14. 18)

"A fortune made by a lying tongue is a fleeting vapor and a deadly snare." (Proverbs 21:6)

"He who oppresses the poor to increase his wealth and he who gives gifts to the rich, both come to poverty."(Proverbs 22:16)

"Whoever loves money never has money enough; whoever loves wealth is never satisfied with his income." (Ecclesiastes 5:10)

"Extortion turns a wise man into a fool, and a bribe corrupts the heart." (Ecclesiastes 7:7).

"Woe to him who builds his palace by unrighteousness,his upper rooms by injustice, making his countrymen work for nothing, not paying them for their labor." (Jeremiah 22:13)

"Why spend money on what is not bread, and your labor on what does not satisfy?" (Isaiah 55:2)

WORK:

"Lazy hands make a man poor, but diligent hands bring wealth." (Proverbs 10:4)

"One who is slack in his work is brother to one who destroys." (Proverbs 18:9)

"He who has been stealing must steal no longer, but must work, doing something useful with his own hands, that he may have something to share with those in need." (Ephesians 4:28)

"For even when we were with you, we gave you this rule: If a man will not work, he shall not eat. Such people we command and urge in the Lord Jesus Christ, to settle down and earn the bread they eat." (II Thessalonians 3:10-12)

"Make it your ambition to lead a quiet life, to mind your own business and to work with your hands, just as we told you." (I Thessalonians 4:11)

SAVINGS:

"Dishonest money dwindles away, but he who gathers money little by little makes it grow." (Proverbs 13:11)

"The man who had received the five talents went at once and put his money to work and gained five more. So also, the one with the two talents gained two more. But the man who had received the one talent went off, dug a hole in the ground and hid his master's money." (Matthew 25:16-18)

GIVING:

"The wicked borrow and do not repay, but the righteous give generously." (Psalms 37:21)

"He who is kind to the poor lends to the Lord, and he will reward him for what he has done."

KNOWLEDGE IS POWER!!

"My people are destroyed for lack of knowledge: because thou hast rejected knowledge, I will also reject thee, that thou shalt be no priest to me: seeing thou hast forgotten the law of thy God, I will also forget thy children." (Hosea 4:6) - King James Version

With the knowledge and understanding that "as a man thinketh in his heart, mind and soul so is he," and fortified with a daily diet of <u>MIND FOOD</u> (Appendix II), the Economic Emancipation Warriors will become a formidable foe on the "economic battlefields" of America.

The <u>Economic Emancipation Plan</u> represents a comprehensive approach to economic self-development of Black America through the Church community by leveraging financial resources and developing business and commercial enterprises, and economic development projects. The underlying philosophy of this Plan is the creation of permanent jobs and employment opportunities in urban and rural communities. The primary focus of this Plan is in three basic areas. They are as follow:

(1) Capital Formation and Accumulation

(2) Business Enterprise Development

(3) Economic Education and Training

One of the major problems faced by Black America is the lack of control over our own financial resources. Our insurance premiums, deposits in majority banks, savings and loan associations, credit unions, and pension programs provide very little, if any, meaningful economic and investment impact in our communities. As a result of this situation, the growth and expansion of Black owned business enterprises and commercial ventures are severely curtailed, thereby limiting and restricting employment opportunities so urgently needed in urban and rural areas across the nation. Investment capital which should and could be made available to local community economic development efforts is put to work outside immediate Black communities, and in many cases, even outside the country. To address this economic inequity, several financial institutions are being developed. They are as follows:

1. The National Church Credit Union

Unity Credit Union will be developed as a church-based financial institution to serve the finacial and credit needs of our people across denominational lines.

Our Goal is to have 5,000 churches and at least ten (10) members from each church or 50,000 individual memberships by December 31, 1995. You and/or your church can join by simply completing a membership application obtained from the National Office of Penny

Lovers of America, Inc. and dropping it in the mail. You can assist our efforts by encouraging your church and friends to join "Unity Credit Union" - The National Church Credit Union.

2. The Self-Insurance Association

In an era of ever-increasing property and casualty/liability insurance premiums, this Self-Insurance Association will greatly benefit our churches and communities. Surplus funds from this Association will be invested in housing, nursing homes, day care centers, and other revenue producing business ventures with employment opportunities.

Our Goal is to have 5,000 churches participating in this Self-Insurance Association by December 31, 1995. Church representatives interested should photocopy Appendix III, page 147, and return completed form to Penny Lovers of America, Inc. for information.

3. The 5-2-1 Fund (A National Development Fund)

The inspiration for this fund came from the Holy Scriptures, Matthew 25:14-30 (The Parable of the Talents). The National Development Fund will be created through voluntary monthly assessments of individual families based on annual family income and by individual churches based upon their membership. The Fund will be managed by a professional asset management company, and Dr. Samuel D. Proctor has been invited to chair the Board of Trustees.

How to Participate
Individual Family/Churches/Organizations
(1)   Determine monthly assessment from chart shown below.

(2)   Send monthly assessment to 5-2-1 Fund, c/o Penny Lovers of America, P.O. Box 6141, Somerset, New Jersey 08875-6141.

(3) Encourage your friends, associates and churches to participate in the 5-2-1 Fund.

(4)   Read Matthew 25:14-30 verses.

Our Goal is to have 100,000 families and 5,000 churches actively participating in the Fund by December 31, 1995.

FAMILY INCOME:
*1989

$0-$7,499	1,572,000 families	(21.2%)
$7,500-$14,999	1,463,000 families	(19.8%)
over $15,000	4,374,000 families	(59.0%)
**Total Families	7,409,000	100.0%

*Source: U.S. Census Bureau
**African-American families

PENNY POWER • PENNY POWER • PENNY POWER

FAMILY ASSESSMENT:

Family Income	Monthly Assessment
$0-7,499	$1.00/family
$7,500-$14,999	$2.00/family
over $15,000	$5.00/family

CHURCH ASSESSMENT:

Church Membership	Monthly Assessment
100 members or less	$5.00/church
over 100 members	$10.00/church

USE OF FUNDS:

(a) Purchase of land
(b) Stock/investments
(c) Education Loan Program

4.College & University Endowment (CUE) Program

Under this component, we propose to develop the College & University Endowment (CUE) Program as a means of financially assisting the Historical Black Colleges and Universities (HBCU). The purpose of the CUE Program is to improve the financial stability of their graduates, and by making it financially attractive and beneficial for graduates to support their alma maters.

Specifically, the objectives of the CUE Program are as follows:

(1) To help college graduates establish and develop realistic short-term and long-range financial goals.

(2) To help college graduates structure sound financial investment programs early in their professional careers that will assure them maximum financial return over the span of their most productive working years.

(3) To help historically Black colleges and universities develop substantially increased endowment income through regular and systematic contributions from their alumni.

We subscribe to the concept that the ever-increasing cost of maintaining institutions of higher learning must be shared in greater proportions in years to come by the products of these institutions--their graduates. This concept is consistent with the philosophy of the free enterprise system which essentially supports the theory that a good business venture is supported and sustained through the marketing of its products and services.

These institutions have made an invaluable contribution to America by serving as a vital source for scientists, computer experts, engineers, lawyers, doctors, nurses, social workers, military officers, teachers, business-men, and responsible leadership of our society.

Horace Mann once stated that
"If ever there was a cause
If ever there can be a cause
Worthy to be upheld by all the toil
or sacrifices that the human
heart can endure,
It is the cause of education."

And Thomas Wolf stated that:
"To every man his chance;
To every man regardless of his birth,
his shining golden opportunity;
To every man the right to live,
to work, to be himself;
To become whatever his manhood and
decisions combine to make him,
That is the promise of America."

For thousands and thousands of African-Americans, education is an important cause and has been the key to a better life. Education has been a way out of the ghettos of the North and the shanties and plantations of the South. Historically Black Colleges and Universities-- both private and public, have provided educational opportunities for hundreds of thousands of African-American students in the fulfillment of the promise of America as stated by Thomas Wolfe. It is in the best interest of all America, and especially Black America, for the continued existence and support of these institutions.

5. The Annual National Penny Campaign

As a people, we need a national symbol which represents both our hopes, aspirations and dreams; and also our hurts, pains and disappointments, and at the same time conveys a simple and basic economic message which challenges and motivates us to unite with a sense of historical and cultural pride, determined to build, develop and progress as a race of people, committed to a "self-help and self-determination philosophy." At first consideration, this need may appear to be an impossibility, with no hope of achieving. However, I deeply believe that my 'vision' of the penny fully meets those parameters. Let's consider the lonely and humble 'penny' for a moment.

First of all, the penny represents our "total color spectrum," from 'high yellow' to 'jet black.' It carries a picture of President Abraham Lincoln, the author of the Emancipation Proclamation and also called the "Emancipator". It is isolated, neglected, abused and discriminated against. For example, how often have you traveled through toll gates on our nation's turnpikes and expressways and observed signs which read--"No pennies, please." Remember the demonstration by Andy Rooney of CBS "60 Minutes" several years ago with a penny, dime and quarter placed on the floor near an escalator in Grand Central Station in New York City. People walked over the penny until it was joined by a dime, and finally a quarter, and then they only stopped to pick up the dime and quarter leaving the penny behind to be further abused by passing trampling feet. What shameful treatment and disrespect of the most important unit of currency in our monetary system. How else do you get to a dollar except you start with a 'penny?' My father always told me "to take care of the pennies, the dollars will take care of themselves."

Symbols are important to a business, a people or a nation. Whether its the NBC peacock; the Star of David for Jews, the Cross for Christians, the Shamrock for the Irish, or the Old Glory--our precious flag--to Americans, symbols are viewed with reverence and respect, or disdain and contempt, depending on one's allegiance, loyalty and philosophy, and the cause for which the symbols represent.

As African-Americans, the 'penny' represents all the things that we have faced as a race of people. Discrimination and segregation; abuse and benign neglect;

isolation and barriers; lack of opportunities for productivity and usefulness are common and shared experiences. We can and do express our hurt, pain and disappointments when confronting these difficulties and barriers. But what about the 'penny?' Have you ever considered how a penny must feel about hope, aspirations and desire to contribute to society?

My personal relationship and affinity for the 'penny' started when I was a youngster. When I was 3 or 4 years old, for some unknown reason, I swallowed 5 pennies. I still remember picking up those pennies from the corner of a foot-pedal sewing machine and swallowing them one after the other. What possessed me to do such a foolish thing, I'll never know. But it was probably the same thing that possessed college students in the sixties to swallow goldfish; crowd in telephone booths; streak stark naked in public places and chug-a-lug beer until they passed out. "The devil made us do it." But seriously, whatever it was, in the spring of 1984--42 years later-- I was awakened around 2:00 a.m. one night from a deep sleep by the hand of God with the inspiration to write the words-- A Penny Speaks. These words expressed by a "penny" itself, convey a burning desire to unite with other non-productive, abused and seemingly worthless pennies to make positive contributions to society and improve the conditions and the quality of life for our people through united "<u>PENNY</u> <u>POWER</u>."

A PENNY SPEAKS

By: Richard E. Barber, Sr.
(Written in 1984)

Give the Penny Lovers of America your isolated, abused and trampled on, lonely and hidden pennies yearning to be loved and useful. You will find us in desks, kitchens and dresser drawers, in closets, behind and under furniture, in shoe boxes, under and between car seats and in piggy banks, forgotten and therefore non-productive. We lead an humble and hermit-like existence, not fully appreciated and therefore not circulated as the other coins. My individual purchasing power is practically nil. What can you buy for a penny today? There's no more penny candy, bubble gum, or baseball and football cards! Children use to want me, but no more. Why do I really exist? What is my purpose in this society? The answer, I believe, is in unity; for in unity, there is strength and through strength there can be great and significant achievements. Therefore, pennies of the world, let us unite and we will become a powerful and creative economic force in this society. Let the pennies come forth from the North, the South, the East and the West. From the great cities of America--New York, Chicago, Milwaukee, Seattle, Portland,

Los Angeles, Boston, Newark, Philadelphia, Pittsburgh, Baltimore, Washington, Richmond, Charlotte, Atlanta, Miami and Orlando, Dallas and Houston, New Orleans and others, to small country towns such as Trenton and Seaboard, North Carolina; villages and sleepy hamlets in Virginia, North and South Carolina, Georgia, Alabama, Florida, Arkansas, Mississippi, Louisiana, Texas, Oklahoma, New Mexico, Kentucky, Ohio and Indiana, Iowa and Wyoming, the Dakotas--all the states and territories. From prison cells to military installations around the globe, let the pennies come!

Let Penny Lovers shout <u>PENNY POWER</u> throughout the land and countryside, across hills and vales, meadows and brooks, mountains and valleys,--from sea to shining sea!

With organized <u>PENNY POWER</u> we will send kids to computer and recreational camps; we will provide scholarships to disadvantaged, under-privileged and handicapped young people; we can bring joy, happiness, and companionship into the lives of senior citizens. United, we represent meaningful community and economic development projects, food, clothing and shelter for the homeless. United, we represent cultural, arts and crafts programs, laughing and happy children in day care centers, educational and training programs for the unemployed and underemployed, and health and human services for our citizens. Yes, there is no limit to what we pennies can do united with a sense of purpose and devoted to an agenda of progress for our people.

So all you Penny Lovers, on your mark, get set, come and get us!!

The message conveyed in this monologue--<u>A Penny Speaks</u>--provides our mission and purpose for our cause to implement a national "grass roots self-help" movement of Economic Emancipation. These efforts are being realized through Penny Lovers of America Inc., a non-profit entity which was organized in 1985.

The logo of Penny Lovers of America, Inc. consists of seven (7) pennies as shown below:

The motto of Penny Lovers of America is:

CHARACTER -SCHOLARSHIP-PATRIOTISM

The meaning of this logo was derived from the Seven (7) Principles developed by Dr. Ron Karenga in the 1960's and graphically displayed on the cover of the Black Scholar Magazine in 1974 as shown on the next page.

A DESIGN OF THE SEVEN PRINCIPLES

A Black Value System and the Seven Principles:

1. Unity - strive for and maintain unity in the family, community, nation and race.
2. Self-Determination - define ourselves, name ourselves, decide on our future.
3. Collective Work and Responsibility - build and maintain our community together and make the problems of our brothers and sisters our own and work to solve them together.
4. Cooperative Economics - build and maintain our stores, shops and other businesses and profit together from them
5. Purpose - make, as our collective vocation, the building and developing of our community to restore our people to their traditional greatness.
6. Creatively - do always as much as we can in such a way that we leave our community more beautiful and beneficial than when we inherited it.
7. Faith - believe with all our hearts in our parents, teachers, leaders and in the righteousness and victory of our struggle.

I am hopeful that supporters of our cause will strive to live the intent of these principles in our efforts to instill a larger vision in the minds of African-Americans on our journey toward Economic Emancipation.

The Annual National Penny Campaign is being Chaired by Mel Blount, former Pittsburgh Steeler and National Football League (NFL) Hall of Famer.

Mel has recruited scores of professional sports figures and entertainers to assist in this national effort. Appendix IV is a copy of the letter of invitation from Mel to professional athletes and entertainers.

The annual national goal is to raise 1,000,000 pounds of pennies ($1,640,000.00) for support of the Economic Emancipation Program, the Mel Blount Youth Home, scholarships, and selected community development projects.

In order to make this national Economic Emancipation initiative within the economic reach of everyone, we have established some very nominal pledge goals for maximum participation. These goals and standards are as follows:

(1) one inch = 17 pennies
(2) one foot = 204 pennies ($2.04) = 1.25
      pounds of pennies
(3) one yard = 612 pennies ($6.12) = 3.75
      pounds of pennies
(4) one mile = 1,077,120 pennies =
      ($10,771.20) = 6600 pounds of pennies

Special Note: 164 pennies = one pound

We are encouraging school children, sports fans, military personnel, prison inmates, individuals, churches, family reunions, clubs and organizations, and the business and corporate community to join this effort by selecting an annual pledge from the goals and standards listed above. Photocopy page 146 and complete the information requested for participation in the National Penny Campaign and commitment to this cause. Return completed form to:

Mel Blount, Chairman
National Penny Campaign
Penny Lovers of America, Inc.
P.O. Box 6141
Somerset, New Jersey 08875-6141

For persons and organizations interested in sponsoring a Penny Party, please photocopy Appendix III and complete the information requested for the Penny Party Information Packet. Return completed form to:

Penny Lovers of America, Inc.
P.O. Box 6141-PPI
Somerset, New Jersey 08875-6141

For churches interested in the Self-Insurance Association, photocopy Appendix III, complete and return to:

Penny Lovers of America, Inc.
P.O. Box 6141-SIA
Somerset, New Jersey 08875-6141

Various methods have been planned to achieve this annual goal. The primary methods are as follows:
1. Certificate of Commitment

We are seeking 100,000 persons who will sign the Certificate of Commitment pledging to support the economic goals and objectives of the Economic Emancipation Plan for a minimum period of five years by saving at least "one penny each day" for this historic "self-help initiative."

Persons wishing to participate should complete the Certificate of Commitment (Appendix V) and return it to Mel Blount with the first year commitment of 365 pennies ($3.65). Check or money order-- no pennies, please, (smile)--made payable to Penny Lovers of America, Inc. Future pledges of $3.65 annually are due on January 15th (Dr. Martin Luther King Jr.'s Birthday).

COMMITMENT

Commitment is what transforms a promise into reality.

It is the words that speak boldly of your intentions. And the actions which speak louder than the words.

Coming through time after time after time, year after year after year.
Commitment is the stuff character is made of; the power to change the face of things.

--Author Unknown

2. Penny Parties

We are seeking hosts and hostesses to hold Penny Parties and invite their friends and neighbors to bring their pennies and pledge to save at least "one penny each day" for this cause. A video explaining the Economic Emancipation Plan featuring the monologue, "A Penny Speaks," narrated by Ossie Davis is available for showing at these parties. Persons interested in hosting a Penny Party should photocopy Appendix III, page 147, and return completed form to Penny Lovers of America, Inc. for a Penny Party Information Packet. Professional athletes and entertainers will be invited to participate in as many of these parties as possible. Hosts and hostesses are needed in every city, town, hamlet, village and crossroads in America where African-Americans and other supporters reside. The one hundred (100) cities with the largest African-American population and the annual penny goals of these cities are as follows:

City/Town	Annual Penny Goal	Annual Goal in Miles*	Annual Goal in Pounds
New York, NY	12,000,000	12	79,200
Chicago, IL	10,000,000	10	66,000
Detroit, MI	8,000,000	8	52,800
Philadelphia, PA	6,000,000	6	39,600
Los Angeles, CA	6,000,000	6	39,600

City/Town	Annual Penny Goal	Annual Goal in Miles*	Annual Goal in Pounds
Washington, DC	5,000,000	5	33,000
Houston, TX	4,000,000	4	28,400
Baltimore, MD	4,000,000	4	28,400
New Orleans, LA	3,000,000	3	19,800
Memphis, TN	3,000,000	3	19,800
Atlanta, GA	3,000,000	3	19,800
Dallas, TX	3,000,000	3	19,800
Cleveland, OH	2,000,000	2	13,200
St. Louis, MO	2,000,000	2	13,200
Newark, NJ	2,000,000	2	13,200
Oakland, CA	2,000,000	2	13,200
Birmingham, AL	2,000,000	2	13,200
Indianapolis, IN	2,000,000	2	13,200
Milwaukee, WI	2,000,000	2	13,200
Jacksonville, FL	2,000,000	2	13,200
Cincinnati, OH	2,000,000	2	13,200
Boston, MA	2,000,000	2	13,200
Columbus, OH	2,000,000	2	13,200
Kansas City, MO	2,000,000	2	13,200
Richmond, VA	2,000,000	2	13,200
Gary, IN	2,000,000	2	13,200
Nashville-Davidson, TN	2,000,000	2	13,200
Pittsburgh, PA	1,000,000	1	6,600
Charlotte, NC	1,000,000	1	6,600
Jackson, MS	1,000,000	1	6,600
Buffalo, NY	1,000,000	1	6,600
Norfolk, VA	1,000,000	1	6,600
Fort Worth, TX	1,000,000	1	6,600
Miami, FL	1,000,000	1	6,600
San Francisco, CA	1,000,000	1	6,600
Shreveport, LA	1,000,000	1	6,600
Louisville, KY	1,000,000	1	6,600
Baton Rouge, LA	1,000,000	1	6,600
San Diego, CA	1,000,000	1	6,600
Dayton, OH	1,000,000	1	6,600
Mobile, AL	1,000,000	1	6,600
Montgomery, AL	1,000,000	1	6,600
Savannah, GA	1,000,000	1	6,600
Flint, MI	1,000,000	1	6,600

City/Town	Annual Penny Goal	Annual Goal in Miles*	Annual Goal in Pounds
East Orange, NJ	1,000,000	1	6,600
Tampa, FL	1,000,000	1	6,600
Rochester, NY	1,000,000	1	6,600
Jersey City, NJ	1,000,000	1	6,600
Toledo, OH	1,000,000	1	6,600
Compton, CA	1,000,000	1	6,600
Denver, CO	500,000	1/2	3,300
Oklahoma City, OK	500,000	1/2	3,300
Columbus, GA	500,000	1/2	3,300
San Antonio	500,000	1/2	3,300
Inglewood, CA	500,000	1/2	3,300
Chattanooga, TN	500,000	1/2	3,300
Winston-Salem, NC	500,000	1/2	3,300
East St. Louis, IL	500,000	1/2	3,300
Akron, OH	500,000	1/2	3,300
Macon, GA	500,000	1/2	3,300
Greensboro, NC	500,000	1/2	3,300
Little Rock, AR	500,000	1/2	3,300
Durham, NC	500,000	1/2	3,300
Portsmouth, VA	500,000	1/2	3,300
Paterson, NJ	500,000	1/2	3,300
Seattle, WA	500,000	1/2	3,300
Hartford, CT	500,000	1/2	3,300
Newport News, VA	500,000	1/2	3,300
Camden, NJ	500,000	1/2	3,300
Beaumont, TX	500,000	1/2	3,300
Tulsa, OK	500,000	1/2	3,300
Austin, TX	500,000	1/2	3,300
Hampton, VA	500,000	1/2	3,300
Trenton, NJ	500,000	1/2	3,300
Raleigh, NC	500,000	1/2	3,300
St. Petersburgh, FL	500,000	1/2	3,300
Kansas City, KS	500,000	1/2	3,300
Long Beach, CA	500,000	1/2	3,300
Columbia, SC	500,000	1/2	3,300
New Haven, CT	500,000	1/2	3,300
Youngstown, OH	500,000	1/2	3,300
Orlando, FL	500,000	1/2	3,300

* *Miles Rounded*

City/Town	Annual Penny Goal	Annual Goal in Miles*	Annual Goal in Pounds
Omaha, NE	500,000	1/2	3,300
Phoenix, AZ	500,000	1/2	3,300
Sacramento, CA	500,000	1/2	3,300
Wilmington, DE	500,000	1/2	3,300
Richmond, VA	500,000	1/2	3,300
Albany, GA	500,000	1/2	3,300
Mount Vernon, NY	500,000	1/2	3,300
Charleston, SC	500,000	1/2	3,300
Fort Lauderdale, FL	500,000	1/2	3,300
East Cleveland, OH	500,000	1/2	3,300
Chesapeake, VA	500,000	1/2	3,300
Wichita, K	500,000	1/2	3,300
Bridgeport, CT	500,000	1/2	3,300
Huntsville, AL	500,000	1/2	3,300
San Jose, CA	500,000	1/2	3,300
Prichard, AL	500,000	1/2	3,300
Grand Rapids, MI	500,000	1/2	3,300
Pontiac, MI	500,000	1/2	3,300

Our Annual National Goal of 1,000,000 pounds of pennies represents 151.5 miles of pennies.

We believe that our national goal and our individual goals for the various cities are both reasonable and achievable. We have chosen as our Annual National Penny Campaign Slogan-"Inch By Inch, It's A Cinch." This slogan came from a quotation by Dr. Robert Schuller, Pastor of Crystal Cathedral of Garden Grove, California, "Inch by inch, anything's a cinch" (Appendix X).

In addition to the Certificates of Commitment, and the Penny Parties, we have contacted the nation's pastors and church leaders requesting their support of the Annual

Penny Campaign. In Mel Blount's appeal letter (Appendix VI), he explained our efforts to encourage at least 100,000 young people each year, ages 6-16, to commit to the principles of the Power of Knowledge Pledge (Appendix VII).

The Power of Knowledge Pledge was published in the Wall Street Journal by the United Technologies Corporation of Hartford, Connecticut in 1979 with the footnote: "What a great day for America if every one of our students signed this pledge. The country would benefit and it wouldn't add a penny to school budgets."

Special Note: Please note the addition of paragraph 8 to this Pledge by this writer, with the permission of the United Technologies Corporation, due to the present drug epidemic and the destructive consequences it is having on our young people, our families, our cities, towns and communities, and our entire nation.

AN APPEAL TO THE CHURCH COMMUNITY

The Economic Emancipation of African-Americans

Let the Church Say, Amen!!

"Where There is no Vision, the People Perish."

Proverbs 29:18

Thank God for the Vision!!

R.E.B.

We are seeking 5,000 progressive churches nationwide to participate in the <u>National Economic Emancipation Program</u> . From the pulpits and pews of these churches, we are hopeful, will emanate a consistent and continuous message of <u>E c o n o m i c Emancipation</u> for our people. The successful implementation of this national initiative will be recorded in history as that period in which African-Americans truly "straightened their backs," and started on the journey toward "economic self-sufficiency."

The economic destiny of African-Americans rests upon the united strengths, commitment, and unrealized potential of the Church. The Black church, as an institution, has played a primary leadership and substantive role in the progress and development of Black America. It has been our "bridge over troubled waters" from slavery until this very moment. In an era of decreasing government resources for community economic development, it is imperative that the church community assume an even greater responsibility for the solutions to some of the social and economic problems plaguing our communities. This drastic state of economic affairs represents an opportunity as well as a challenge. It provides an opportunity for the church community to take the initiative and active leadership in developing and implementing an economic 'self-help' program which will directly address the employment and business enterprise development needs of our communities.

As church leaders and assorted "pew warmers", we are collectively challenged to demonstrate that African-Americans can be masters of their own fate. But to achieve a greater degree of self-dependency, we must develop a far more intelligent use of our own resources, both financial and human, to achieve any solid and lasting progress.

Now African-Americans are facing the last frontier and major barrier to full participation in the mainstream of America--that being the economic and financial marketplace. Now is the time for us to prepare to enter the 21st century with our economic agenda in the forefront.

Have we considered that in recent years immigrant groups have come 5,000 or 10,000 miles to our neighborhoods across this nation to establish economic beachheads while we were "asleep at the throttle?" These groups fully recognize, understand and appreciate the 300 billion dollar consumer market in Black America (see Appendix VIII).

Now is the time for us to fulfill the 'Dream' of which Dr. Martin Luther King, Jr. so eloquently spoke some 27 years ago at the Lincoln Memorial in Washington. Now is the time for church leadership to declare that we do indeed support the <u>Economic Emancipation</u> of <u>African-Americans</u>. Now is the time for us to fully accept the commands of God and tell the 'economic pharaohs' of this nation to "let our people go!" Now is the time to demonstrate our understanding and wisdom gained from Proverbs 29:18, "Where there is no vision, the people perish."

I believe, and believe very strongly, that one generation of African-Americans will have to sacrifice their time, talents and energies, and a small portion of their financial resources in order to build productive and meaningful economic institutions for future generations. I ask the question of us today, why not our generation?

To my fellow Christian brethren, "Please don't let this harvest pass." Generations to come will disdain the memory of our names if we fail to seize this opportunity and economically prepare for their future now! Collectively, the Black Church has too much economic potential and job creation strength for our communities to be plagued with double digit unemployment, economic deprivation and a sense of hopelessness. We teach and preach in our churches that "we serve a great and mighty God," and we do. We teach and preach in our churches that "the cattle on a thousand hills belongs to him," and they do. We teach and preach in in our churches that "my Father is rich in houses and land, he holds the wealth of the world in the palm of his hand," and I believe that. However, when we observe the poverty of our people, when we review our history in this nation, and we see how we as a people stack up on the economic ladder, when we consider that Black America, generation after generation, continues to serve as the 'economic footstool' for immigrant groups who come to America, the question very honestly and seriously must be asked, Why is Black America so poor economically? Each of us may have our own answer to that question. But the fact of the matter is that not withstanding the Emancipation Proclamation in 1863, abolishing legal slavery, we as a people still find ourselves in 'economic slavery' even in

1990, one hundred and twenty-seven (127) years later. How long Oh God, how long? How long before we as a people fully understand that if our problems, be they economic, political, educational, or social, are going to be solved, we are going to have to solve them ourselves. We cannot and should not realistically expect other people to solve our problems. If history is any teacher, then I have learned that, in general, and with few exceptions, other ethnic groups may have no vested interest in our economic well-being and independence, except from a self-interest perspective. It is for these reasons that I invite you to become a part of " this economic beginning in Black America"and become a full participating partner with history. So that one hundred years from now, when the generation of the year 2090 asks the question, "where were we and what part did we play in the Economic Emancipation Program," let history record that we answered the call to bear economic arms and we went forth, and "fought a good fight." Let history record that we fully accepted this challenge and went forth into America's economic battlefield with the "courage of David, the faith of Abraham , and the commitment and determination of Nehemiah," knowing full well that we were not alone in this historic effort.

As we move closer to the year 2000, just ten (10) short years away, let us keep the words of our beloved Dr. Martin Luther King, Jr. in mind. He so lovingly said:

> "The belief that God will do everything for man is as untenable as the belief that man can do everything for himself. It, too, is based on lack of faith. We must learn that to expect God to do everything while we do nothing is not faith, but superstition."

With a sense of space age urgency and in the knowledge that "it was not raining when Noah built the ark, " what should we as African-Americans be doing now to help ourselves and to improve our communities?" What should be our overall national goals?

My purpose in developing the <u>Economic Emancipation Plan for African-Americans</u> is to <u>chart</u> a new direction for Black America toward 'self-sufficiency and self-dependency,' and away from a 'welfare mentality and state.' As far as our overall national goals are concerned, a concensus was reached by African-American civil rights, political, business, and education leaders during an April 1989 Economic Summit in New Orleans on the following Year 2000 goals for the economic, educational and political empowerment of African-Americans. The desire of these leaders is that these goals be adopted by the entire African-American community. <u>The Economic Emancipation Plan for African-Americans</u>, as I have outlined in this publication, will greatly assist our national efforts in achieving the Year 2000 goals just ten (10) years away. These goals are as follows:

ECONOMIC EMPOWERMENT

African-Americans will represent 10% of the total wealth in the nation. (currently 3%)

African-Americans will own 12% of the total number of businesses in America. (currently 4%)

African-Americans will spend 36% of their income with other African-Americans. (currently 7%)

African-Americans' income will represent 11% of the total U.S. income. (currently 7%)

African-Americans will have a poverty rate of 13% of its total population. (currently 31%)

EDUCATIONAL EMPOWERMENT

African-Americans (students) will have an individually combined (English/Math) Scholastic Aptitude Test (S.A.T.) score of 1000. (currently 715)

POLITICAL EMPOWERMENT

African-Americans will have 22 million of its population registered to vote. (currently 12 million)

African-Americans will have 20 million of its population actually voting. (currently 10 million)

African-Americans will have 27,000 elected officials. (currently 6600)

Generations unborn will praise the leaders and participants of this effort who had the vision, the courage, the determination to undertake this historic Economic Emancipation initiative as a means of forever eliminating the economic bonds and shackles from the hearts, minds and bodies of African-Americans. These committed leaders and participants became, in the words of the late and great civil rights warrior, Mrs. Fannie Lou Hamer of Mississippi, "sick and tired of being sick and tired" of the perennial status quo and welfare dependency so prevalent in Black America and decided that "enough is enough."

The Golden Rule

"He who has the gold, rules"

CONCLUSION

As I conclude this message, and challenge African-Americans to join this cause of <u>Economic Emancipation</u>, I am reminded of a story of a French nobleman. The story goes that this Frenchman was watching his gardener from his chateau meticulously attending to the shrubbery and flower beds and carefully manicuring the lawn in a particular section of the estate grounds. Later that afternoon as he was driving from the estate, he stopped to ask the gardener how long it would take to do all the grounds as he had this particular section. The gardener remarked, "about 200 years." "Good" replied the nobleman, "get started at once."

If the question were asked of me, "how long will it take for African-Americans to achieve Economic Emancipation," my answer would probably be, "I really don't know, but I do know that it is imperative that we get started <u>at</u> <u>once</u>"

I seriously got started one spring night in March of 1967 in Huntsville, Alabama. I sat in my Bachelor Officers Quarters (BOQ) reflecting on my five (5) year military career which would come to a close on June 1, 1967, just three (3) months hence, and what would I do with the rest of my life. To what causes would I support? How could I use my time and talents to help right some of the wrongs in our nation? What contributions could I make in our struggle as a people for full and equitable participation in the 'American Dream'? I reflected on key events during that five-year period and the impact those events had on me. I thought about my graduation from North Carolina A&T College in 1962 and my being commissioned as a Second Lieutenant in the U.S. Army Ordnance Corps and a Distinguished Military Graduate. I thought about July 18, 1962, my very first day on active duty at Aberdeen Proving Grounds in Maryland, and how I was refused service at several local restaurants, notwithstanding the fact that I had just taken an oath to "uphold and defend the Constitution of these United States." I thought about my marriage to that young nursing graduate, Betty J. Witherspoon, from North Carolina A&T--on September 30, 1962-- and then a registered nurse at Fort Howard V.A. Hospital in Maryland. We were married as James Meredith was trying to enroll in the University of Mississippi which caused a riot, and President Kennedy had to dispatch federal troops to protect Meredith and quell the riot. I remembered with great pleasure the nine-day voyage on the troop transport ship--General Patton--accompanied by my young bride enroute to my first military duty assignment in Zweibrucken, Germany, in March 1963. I then remembered the shameful racial incidents and the tragic events at home during

1963 which caused me to seriously question why I was in the Army 5,000 miles from home, when the real battle was back in the States with the civil rights forces against the 'age old barriers' of discrimination, segregation and unjust restrictions of persons of African-American descent.

I remembered the racial incident at the Heidelburg Officers Club in June of 1963 where four white American military officers entered the club dressed as KKK Klansmen--this was truly an insult to all African-American military personnel serving our country around the globe. I remembered with a heavy heart June 12, 1963, when Medgar Evers, Field Director of the NAACP in Mississippi, was shot down in his driveway while his wife and children looked on in horror. I remembered with pride the March on Washington on August 28, 1963, when Dr. Martin L. King, Jr. stood at the foot of the Lincoln Memorial and told the nation of "his Dream."

I remembered with sadness the morning after those " four little Black angels" were killed by dynamite on September 15, 1963, while sitting in a Sunday School class in the Sixteenth Street Baptist Church in Birmingham, Alabama, when Sgt. Robert Jackson, my platoon sergeant, came to my office and informed me that Denise McNair, "one of those little angels," was his niece. He sat before my desk and wept--and I cried.

I remembered November 22, 1963, with a great sense of personal loss when as the duty officer of the day I received word that President Kennedy had been shot in Dallas, Texas.

I remembered the riot in Detroit, the demonstrations and civil disorders in our cities and towns--across America. I reflected on the needless loss of life and the destruction of property. I remembered and reflected on the lunch counter sit-ins and picketing in Greensboro, North Carolina, in 1960 and my own participation while a student at A&T.

I remembered the "hippie movement" and the rebellious young people of my generation in the early sixties-- the marches and demonstrations--the freedom rides, the rejection of traditional values, the conflict and break-up of families with the rise in cults and other seemingly attractive options for young people.

I remembered that seemingly senseless war in Vietnam where many of our young men and women were either killed or physically maimed or psychologically damaged for life.

As I sat in the quietness of my quarters that March 1967 night and reflected--and remembered the events, the crises, the protests, the conflicts of that period in our history--a period in retrospect when it seemed in short, that "America had lost her way." I was inspired to write some words entitled,

<u>Before</u> <u>I</u> <u>Die</u>,which represent my philosophy and personal ministry and crusade.

Before I Die
By: Richard E. Barber, Sr.
(Written in March 1967)

Before I die:

- I want to drink from the fountain of freedom and pass the cup to future generations.

- I want to inhale the sweet air of liberty and breathe new life and hope into a faltering people.

- I want to replace promise with performance, and replace rhetoric with results.

- I want to push back the dark jungles of suspicion that tend to separate men.

- I want to remove barriers of distrust and unite men in a common cause.

- I want to conquer new horizons with love so that God's will can truly be done on earth.

- I want to silence the guns on foreign battlefields and promote understanding and brotherhood among nations.

- I want to extend the frontiers of freedom so that people the world over may have the freedom of choice.

- I want to pick up the pieces of the shattered dreams of our youth and mold them into a living reality.

- I want to comfort some worried and disillusioned mother when her spirits are low and burdens heavy.

- I want to instill pride and respect in some alcoholic and disrespecting father.

- I want to rekindle the love of God in the hearts of men and return mankind to God's paradise.

Finally, as a 13-year-old farm boy, down in the tobacco belt of North Carolina, I came across some words by the author Everett Hale entitled I Am Only One. These words have been the guiding force of my life--both personal, business and professional life. I strongly encourage the supporters of The Economic Emancipation Plan for African-Americans to take these words to heart, and commit them not only to your lips, but in your hearts, and pledge that your future actions, deeds and efforts will be guided by these words as we walk together this journey toward <u>Economic Emancipation</u>. These words simply are:

I am only one, but I am one;
I cannot do everything, but I can do some things;
and that which I can do, I ought to do;
and that which I ought to do,
By the Grace of God, I will do.

THE DEVELOPMENT OF NEW WORLD NATIONAL BANK
"An Idea Whose Time Had Come"
The Pittsburgh Church Community in Action

In the Introduction and Acknowledgement section of this book, I referred to the development and organizing efforts of New World National Bank in 1975 with the Pittsburgh Church Community in the primary leadership role. Because of the historic involvement and commitment of an entire church community to an economic development initiative, I believe it is of utmost importance and appropriate to highlight the outstanding efforts of a united church community demonstrating their "collective economic clout" in the organizing of a financial institution.

In June of 1973, shortly after I had been elected Chairman of the Board of the organizing group of New World National Bank, I asked Bishop Roy C. Nichols of the United Methodist Church and Dr. David Shannon, Dean of the Pittsburgh Theological Seminary to host a breakfast of the entire Pittsburgh church community leadership including the Catholic and Episcopal Dioceses and the Jewish Community. Approximately forty-five (45) church leaders attended representing most of the religious denominations in the Pittsburgh area. A complete and detailed briefing was conducted on the goals and objectives of our organizing group and the need for a minority-owned financial institution. A Steering Committee was organized under the leadership of Dr.Brannon J. Hopson, Pastor of Mt. Olive Baptist Church in Rankin, Pennsylvania, and history was in the making. Over the next eighteen (18) months, the church community raised $600,000.00 of the $800,000.00 needed to capitalize New World National Bank. Due to the enthusiastic leadership and support of the church community, a cross-section of the entire Pittsburgh community became involved, including professional athletes, Block clubs, sororities and fraternities, the local chapter of the National Postal Alliance, other Federal and state employees, community organizations, civic and professional groups, and the private corporate sector and foundation community. Finally on St. Patrick's Day, March 17, 1975, New World National Bank held its grand opening with a tremendous crowd of supporters, local and national dignitaries attending. I read the following statement on behalf of the Board of Directors, officers and staff of the bank.

"In recent years, minority economic development, as a concept and policy, has increasingly occupied the energies of public and private organizations. The rising consciousness of Black Americans, which had provided the substance and thrust for the social and political achievements of the Civil Rights Movement of the 1960's focused this restless energy to the area of economic development. Recognizing that economic potential was the essential counterpart to the ultimate objective of the Civil Rights Movement, efforts turned to the building of economic institutions.

It was this consciousness and realization, which in the fall of 1971, brought six men of different backgrounds, professional and business interests, together to discuss the formation of a minority controlled bank in Pittsburgh. Realizing the difficult task of organizing a bank, we sought to rally a cross-section of people from all walks of life to support our efforts. The church communities of Pittsburgh, both black and white, heard our call and successfully spearheaded this most important project. They are to be commended for their outstanding efforts and rightfully deserve the credit for our being here today. Professional athletes, the Postal Alliance, Block clubs, sororities and fraternities, community organizations, civic and professional groups, and the general public responded enthusiastically. The opening of New World National Bank which we celebrate today, is the result of the dedicated efforts, untiring determination and prayers of that cross-section of people.

Notwithstanding the energies expended and the seemingly insurmountable difficulties we may have encountered during the organizing stages, we fully realize that the real test of our ability to manage and develop a viable financial institution begins today. Therefore, we call upon the corporate and business community, foundations, labor unions, professional, civic and community groups, and the general public to support New World National Bank. As the bank develops into a strong financial institution, it will have a positive impact on the total Pittsburgh community.

In addition to the economic significance of New World National Bank, images are quite important in a community, especially from the standpoint of youth. Historically, the image that most youth, whether black or white, have had of a banker is that of a middle aged, white man with a white shirt and a dark suit and tie. As small as it might seem, with all of the other changing images, New World National Bank presents a different image--at least in color. Little boys and girls, both black and white, will now realize that bankers come in different colors too.

Approximately 6,000 persons, many of whom for the first time in their lives, now own stock in a commercial bank and they too are now interested in par value, earnings per share, and other financial terms once foreign to them. Now they have a stake in the local economy, in a substantial way that has direct meaning to them. A void had been filled and this is good for the total community.

We are deeply grateful to Equibank for its technical assistance during the last three years, and especially its Chairman, M. A. Cancelliere. His cooperation and willingness to help develop a minority enterprise have been most encouraging. We also express our thanks to Mellon Bank, Keystone Bank, Union National Bank and Pittsburgh National Bank for their donations of furniture, bank equipment, and other bank items. We express a special thanks to Herman Israel, President of Keystone Bank, who was instrumental in our obtaining this facility.

To Mrs. Rita Jones of Hazelwood, an accomplished artist, for donating this beautiful painting which hangs in our lobby, our sincere thanks.

Finally, we express our thanks and gratitude to the news media for its fine coverage of this project. We are hopeful that this cordial relationship continues as we strive to develop New World National Bank into a viable financial institution."

New World National Bank (now the Heritage National Bank) stands proudly as a living monument and testimony of a dedicated and committed church community and serves as a "national model" for the national church community to emulate. It is my hope that our efforts to implement the "<u>Economic Emancipation Plan for African-Americans</u>," with the church community in the "forefront," will achieve new economic horizons for our people.

The following is a pictorial review of the development of New World National Bank.

A PICTORAL REVIEW

OF

THE DEVELOPMENT

OF

NEW WORLD NATIONAL BANK

New World National Bank
downtown Pittsburgh, March 17, 1975.

Bishop Roy C. Nichols (left); Dr. Brannon J. Hopson (center), and Bishop Charles H. Foggie participated in the initial press conference at Central Baptist Church in September 1973 announcing the development of New World National Bank.

Bank directors, Dr. Hopson (left) and Barber (center)
review program activities with Rev. Lee Hicks, Executive Director
of Christian Associates of Western Pennsylvania.

Church Women conduct the Bank Telethon (seated from left to right) Mrs. Catherine Graham of Central Baptist Church; Mrs. Irene Nicholson of the AME Zion Church; Mrs. Ruth Bailey of Metropolitan Baptist Church;
Mrs. Mary Ellen Lea of Mt. Ararat Baptist Church;
and Mrs. Ethel D. Grandy of Metropolitan Baptist Church;
standing (left) are Mrs. Johnnie Bell Hopson and Mrs. Ora Sims Watson. (Not shown: Mrs. Katie Everett Johnson).

Mrs. Fannie Royston (seated) and Mrs Nellie Blair making calls during the Bank Telethon.

Bank directors (from left to right) Hopson, Burks, Glenn, Barber, Onyondo, and Nickens discuss the Open-House activities.

Gladys McNairy (center) Chairperson of New World National
Bank Telethon Committee poses with supporters
Frank and Nancy Bolden.

Stage and screen star Abbey Lincoln (center) assisted bank personnel with promotional activities.

Professional athletes Willie Stargell (left) of the Pittsburgh
Pirates, Roy Jefferson of the Washington Redskins and former
Pittsburgh Steeler (2nd from left), and Al Oliver of the Pittsburgh
Pirates join hands with Barber symbolizing their support of New
World National Bank.

Father Phillip J. Haggerty (seated left) presents a $20,000.00 check to Dr. Brannon J. Hopson, bank director as the Roman Catholic investment in the bank as Dick Barber and Father Joseph A. Duchene, provincial treasurer look on.

Pittsburgh Pirates' pitching ace Doc Ellis (left) and Al Oliver, star outfielder chat with Barber and Attorney Tom Reich.

Barber welcomes Norma Madden (center), Executive Assistant to Governor Milton Shapp and Faye Johnson, local business owner to the Open-House celebration.

Barber welcomes Mrs. Myrlie Evers to the Recognition Banquet sponsored by the bank.

Television personality Sir John Christian, a strong bank supporter chats with Barber at the reception.

Popular stage star Nancy Wilson (center), took time from her busy
schedule to endorse "Stand-Up-and-Be-Counted Day" for
New World National Bank, and to assist Mrs. Willa Mae Rice (left)
and Mrs. Gladys McNairy in urging local women's groups to
champion the efforts of the bank.

Popular WAMO radio personality Bill Powell poses with Barber after interview with singing star Nancy Wilson.

Barber greets M.A. Cancelliere (left) Chairman of Equibank, and John O'Connor, Secretary of the Pennsylvania Department of Commerce at the bank grand opening celebration.

The National Bank charter is proudly displayed by Board Chairman Barber (center), Ralph Jones, President, and James Wade, Secretary of Administration and Governor Shapp's representative to the bank opening.

Wesley Posvar, Chancellor of the University of Pittsburgh, chats with Barber during the bank reception.

Congressman William Moorhead was given a bank tour
by Dick Barber.

The executive team - Barber, Chairman (center), Robert Muth (left), Executive Vice-President, and Ralph Jones, President.

Bank supporters Ralph and Sylvia Burnett,
and a fellow stockholder celebrate with
Barber during the Open-House activities.

Hostess for the grand opening celebration from left to right, Cecilia Samuels, Vicky Henderson, Ruth Hall and Marie Chavis pose for the camera.

Barber and fellow banker Elias Ngeleski (right), Financial
Manager of the Tanzania National Bank of Commerce participate
in a WAMO radio show hosted by Derrick Hill.

Herman Israel, President of Keystone Bank and a staunch
supporter of efforts to establish New World Bank welcomes
Barber to his office.

Grand Worthy Matron Sara Dillard Austin and Grand Worthy
Patron Robert L. Smith of the Order of the Eastern Star presents a
$5,000.00 check to Barber to open their account during the 59th
Session of Deborah Grand Chapter held in Philadelphia in 1975.

PENNY POWER • PENNY POWER • PENNY POWER

An evening of entertainment and relaxation for Barber and wife, Betty; bank director William Glenn and wife Mildred; and Brady Keys Jr.; President of the Keys Group and former Pittsburgh Steeler, and wife Anna.

PENNY POWER • PENNY POWER • PENNY POWER

Johnny Ford, Mayor of Tuskeegee, Alabama congratulates Barber on the opening of the bank.

Lou Mason. President of the City Council brought greetings on behalf of the City.

Allegheny County Commissioner Tom Foerster makes history as he opens the first personal checking account in New World National Bank as head teller Cecilia Samuels assists.

Directors, Dr. Hopson (left) and Bill Glenn (right), join Barber in promoting the bank's Christmas Club.

Barber smiles broadly after having cut the ribbon at the grand
opening celebration.

The preceding Pictorial Review is only a bird's-eye overview of the enthusiasm, the intense pride and commitment, and the determined resolve of a cross-section of the Pittsburgh community - with the church leaders in the forefront - to establish New World National Bank - "an idea whose time had come." When the development and history of New World National Bank is researched indepth and accurately written by some historian in years to come, the names of Bishop Roy C. Nichols; Bishop Charles H. Foggie; Bishop Vincent Leonard; Bishop Appleyard; Dr. Brannon J. Hopson; Rev. Isaac Green; Rev. Elmer Williams; Rev. J.A, Williams; Dr. David T. Shannon; Rev. Alfred Pugh;

Rev. Ira Lavigne; Rev. C.L. Pryor; Rev. W.D. Petett; Rev. J. Van Winsett; Rev. L.L. Jefferson; Rev. E.D. Davis; Rev. Carl Moncreiff; Rev. George Kendall; Rev. C.H. Byars; Rev. Norman Johnson; Rev. Jesse McFarland; Rev. H.S. Cuff; Rev. David L. Jemison; Rev. H. Beecher Hicks; Rev. Howard Amos; Rev. W. Lee Hicks; Dr. Leroy Patrick; Rev. John Venable; Rev. Canon Junius Carter; Rev. Leroy Walker; Rev. Rufus Arterberry; Rev. Donald Tunie; Rev. George L. Bowick; Rev. Ted Pollard; Rev. C.W. Torrey; Rev. M. Strong; Rev. D.D. Chatman; Rev. R.W. Twiggs; Rev. R.M. Reeves; Rev. Charles Kirkland; Rev. A.L. Hardaway; Rev. Asa Roberts; Rev. Donald Turner; Rev. Samson Cooper; Rev. C. Carter; Rev. L.G. Cox; Rev. Richard Jones; Rev. A.A. Henderson; Rev. M. Barron; Rev. S.D. Bonaparte; Rev. M.W. Burnett;

Rev. Jezreel Toliver; Rev. C. Leroy Hacker; Rev. Ralph Weems; Rev. Eugene Roberts; Rev. Clifton Ruggs; Rev. W.C. Burnett; Rev. Bishop Thompson; Rev. B.S. Mason; Rev. R.W. Martin and other church leaders and lay persons whose names are a permanent part of the bank's archives - shall be indelibly etched throughout the pages of that history. These church leaders established a new standard of stewardship for the nation's churches and religious institutions by their leadership and advocacy role in community and economic development. Generations to come will owe a great debt of gratitude to these individuals who - by their commitment and sacrifice - instilled the spirit of self-reliance and knowledge in the hearts and minds of Pittsburghers that financial institutions are an integral part of our liberation and freedom. I am grateful to God to have been a part of that movement which shall bear fruits for generations yet unborn.

THE PENALTY OF LEADERSHIP

In every field of human endeavor, he that is first must perpetually live in the white light of publicity. Whether the leadership be vested in a man or in a manufactured product, emulation and envy are ever at work. In art, in literature, in music, in industry, the reward and punishment are always the same. The reward is widespread recognition; the punishment, fierce denial and detraction. When a man's work becomes a standard for the whole world, it also becomes a target for the shafts of the envious few. If his work be merely mediocre, he will be left severely alone--if he achieves a masterpiece, it will set a million tongues a-wagging. Jealousy does not protrude its forked tongue at the artist who produces a commonplace painting. Whatsoever you write, or paint, or play, or sing, or build, no one will strive to surpass or to slander you, unless your work be stamped with the seal of genius. Long, long after a great work or a good work has been done, those who are disappointed or envious continue to cry out that it cannot be done. Spiteful little voices in the domain of art were raised against our own Whistler as a mountebank, long after the big world had acclaimed him its greatest artistic genius. Multitudes flocked to Bayreuth to worship the musical shrine of Wagner, while the little group of those whom he had dethroned and displaced argued angrily that he was no musician at all. The little world continued to protest that Fulton could never build a steamboat, while the big world flocked to the river banks to see his boat stream by. The leader is assailed because he is a leader, and the effort to equal him is merely added proof of that leadership. Failing to equal or to excel, the follower seeks to depreciate and to destroy-- but only confirms once more the superiority of that which he strives to supplant.

There is nothing new in this. It is as old as the world and as old as the human passions-- envy, fear, greed, ambition, and the desire to surpass. And it all avails nothing. If the leader truly leads, he remains--the leader. Master-poet, master-painter, master-workman, each in his turn is assailed, and each holds his laurels through the ages. That which is good or great makes itself known, no matter how loud the clamor of denial. That which deserves to live--lives.

This text appeared as an advertisement in The Saturday Evening Post, January 2nd, in the year 1915.
Copyright, Cadillac Motor Car Company

MIND FOOD

1. Nothing will ever be attempted if all possible objections must first be overcome.

    Dr. Samuel Johnson

2. "I must do something" will solve more problems than "Something must be done."

3. It doesn't do you any good to sit up and take notice if you keep on sitting.

MIND FOOD

4.   Don't let the part that you can't do all you want to do, keep you from doing what you can do.

Francois De Salignac

5.   There is no limit to what can be accomplished if it doesn't matter who gets the credit.

6.   Many people have the right aim in life - but they just never pull the trigger.

MIND FOOD

7. Keep in step with yourself and you need not worry about the rest of the parade.

   Oscar Wilde

8. There is only one proof of ability - action.

   Marie Ebner-Eschenbach

9. When you're average, you're as close to the bottom as you are to the top.

MIND FOOD

10. Out of the lowest depths there is a path to the loftiest height.

   Thomas Carlyle

11. When you have reached the end of your rope, there is only one thing left to do - start climbing!

12. Anybody who has the mind to do it can - so it's having the mind for it that counts.

MIND FOOD

13. Almost everyone knows the difference between right and wrong. But some just hate to make decisions.

14. Charity begins at home, but it degenerates into selfishness if it does not include all homes.

15. Cooperation is not a sentiment - it is an economic necessity.

MIND FOOD

16.   It is not enough just to put your shoulder to the wheel, you must push.

17.   Life does not require us to make good; it asks only that we give our best at each new level of experience.

Harold W. Ruoff

18.   Unless a man undertakes more than he can possibly do he will never do all that he can.

MIND FOOD

19. The best preparation for tomorrow is to live fully today.

20. One generation plants the trees...another gets the shade.

Chinese Proverb

21. True charity is not to give to the needy, but to see to it that there are no needy.

Constancio C. Vigil

MIND FOOD

22. The man who thinks he has arrived is already slipping.

William Feather

23. What you are is God's gift to you; what you make of yourself is your gift to Him.

24. When God allows a burden to be upon you, He will put His own arm underneath you to help.

MIND FOOD

25. If everyone gives one thread, the poor man will have a shirt.

Russian Proverb

26. God promises a safe landing but not a calm passage.

Bulgarian Proverb

27. The only way to live is to accept each minute as an unrepeatable miracle, which is exactly what it is - a miracle and unrepeatable.

MIND FOOD

28. If I cannot do great things, I can do small things is a great way.

James Freeman Clarke

29. Work is more than a way of earning a living - it's a way of keeping one's self-respect.

30. To be ignorant of the past is to remain a child.

MIND FOOD

31. We review the past, not in order to return to it but that we may find in what direction it points to the future.

    Calvin Coolidge

32. Wealth may not guarantee happiness, but neither does poverty.

33. The voice of the majority is no proof of justice.

    Johann Christoph
    Friedrich Von Schiller

MIND FOOD

34.   No money is the root of all evil.

Ilka Chase

35.   Money is like fertilizer - What good is it unless you spread it around?

36.   The use of money is all the advantage there is in having it.

Benjamin Franklin

<u>MIND FOOD</u>

37. There will always be a frontier where there
     is an open mind and a willing hand.

                              Charles Kettering

38. Have patience. All things are difficult
     before they become easy.

                              Saadi

39. It is people that count; you want to put
     yourself into people; they touch other
     people; these still others; and so you go on
     working forever.

                              Alice Freeman Palmer

MIND FOOD

40. Only those who have the patience to do simple things perfectly will acquire the skill to do difficult things easily.

Johann Christoph Von Schiller

41. Skill to do comes of doing.

Ralph Waldo Emerson

42. With ordinary talent and extraordinary perseverance, all things are attainable.

Thomas Fowell Buxton

MIND FOOD

43. The man who wins may have been counted out several times, but he didn't hear the referee.

H.E. Jansen

44. Wishing consumes as much energy as planning.

45. Poverty is death in another form.

Latin Proverb

MIND FOOD

46. Poverty is the greatest social evil from which all others spring. Poverty creates envy between countries and covetousness of each other's possessions; it sets individual against individual and nation against nation.

John Kotetawala

47. Any jackass can kick a barn down, but it takes a carpenter to build one.

President Lyndon Johnson

48. The most acceptable service of God is doing good to men.

MIND FOOD

49.   All glory comes from daring to begin.

50.   They can conquer who believe they can.

Virgil

51.   It is easier to pull down than to build.

Latin Proverb

MIND FOOD

52. He who lends to the poor gets his interest from God.

German Proverb

53. Progress - the onward stride of God.

Victor Hugo

54. There are only two families in the world, the Haves and the Have-Nots.

MIND FOOD

55. Social progress does not have to be bought at the price of individual freedom.

John Foster Dulles

56. There is no point in our ancestors speaking to us unless we know how to listen.

Mortimer J. Adler

57. It is ideas, not vested interests, which are dangerous for good or evil.

John Maynard Keyes

MIND FOOD

58. Without frugality none can be rich, and with it very few would be poor.

59. Let him that would move the world, first move himself.

Socrates

60. No army can withstand the strength of an idea whose time has come.

Victor Hugo

To the Economic Emancipation warriors and supporters, I strongly recommend and encourage you to nourish your mind daily with <u>Mind Food</u> so that your determination and commitment will continually motivate you to positive and constructive actions as we collectively work for the achievement of Economic Emancipation of African-Americans

Special note:
Quotations 1 - 46 under the caption <u>Mind Food</u> were taken from the <u>Lifetime Speaker's Encyclopedia, Volume I, Jacob M. Braude, Prentice-Hall.</u>

Quotations 48 -60 under the caption <u>MIND FOOD</u> were taken from The Public Speaker's Treasure Chest, Herbert V. Prochnow and Herbert V. Prochnow, Jr., Harper & Row, Publishers.

THE NATIONAL PENNY CAMPAIGN
"Inch by Inch It's a Cinch"

Individuals
Dear Mel:

I, _____ of _____
City _____ State _____ Zip Code _____
pledge _____ inch(es), _____ feet, _____ yard(s), or
_____ pounds of pennies annually to support the Economic Emancipation Program, the Mel Blount Youth Home; scholarships and selected community development projects.

Signed _____

THE NATIONAL PENNY CAMPAIGN
"Inch by Inch It's a Cinch"

Churches, Clubs and Organizations/Family Reunions
Dear Mel;

The _____ located at _____
City _____ State _____ Zip Code _____
pledges _____ inch(es), _____ feet, _____ yard(s),
_____ mile(s), or _____ pounds of pennies annually to support the Economic Emancipation Program, the Mel Blount Youth Home; scholarships and selected community development projects.

Signed _____

THE NATIONAL PENNY CAMPAIGN
"Inch by Inch It's a Cinch"

Corporations/Businesses
Dear Mel;

The _____ located at _____
City _____ State _____ Zip Code _____
pledges ___ yard(s), ___ 1/8 mile, _____ 1/4 mile, _____
1/2 mile, _____ full mile(s), or _____ pounds of pennies annually to support the Economic Emancipation Program, the Mel Blount Youth Home; scholarships and selected community development projects.

Signed _____

PENNY POWER • PENNY POWER • PENNY POWER

APPENDIX III
SELF-INSURANCE ASSOCIATION

Our church is interested in the Self-Insurance Association for churches. Please send me complete information.

Name _____

Church _____

Address _____

City _____ State_____ Zip_____

Telephone No.: Area Code (___) _____

PENNY PARTY INFORMATION PACKET

Dear Mel:

I am interested in hosting a Penny Party in (City/Town)_____

_____.

Name _____

Address _____

City _____ State_____ Zip_____

Telephone No.: Area Code (___) _____

PENNY POWER • PENNY POWER • PENNY POWER

APPENDIX IV

Dear Fellow Athletes/Entertainers:

As professional athletes and entertainers, we have a very profound and serious obligation to provide a positive influence to millions of young people who idolize us as hero figures. In this regard, I am writing to request your personal participation in the Annual National Penny Campaign.

The Annual National Penny Campaign is sponsored by the Penny Lovers of America, Inc., a non-profit organization based in Somerset, New Jersey. The primary purpose and mission of Penny Lovers of America, Inc. is to convey a message of <u>Character-Building</u>, <u>Scholarship</u>, and <u>Patriotism</u> to the young people of America, ages 6-16. I have been asked by the Board of Directors of Penny Lovers of America to serve as Chairman of the National Penny Campaign. I have consented to do so, and I am now recruiting fellow athletes and entertainers to assist me in this most worthwhile national effort.

Our national goal is to raise 1,000,000 pounds of pennies ($1,640,000.00) annually or 151.5 miles of pennies for scholarships and selected community development projects annually, and to encourage participants to save "one penny each day" for the Penny Lovers organization on an on-going basis. The attached monologue entitled <u>A Penny Speaks</u>, by a penny itself provides our charge and reasons for this National Penny Campaign.

Our second goal is to encourage at least 100,000 young people each year to commit to the principles of the <u>Power of Knowledge Pledge</u> (see attached) and sign it along with a parent/or guardian, and one of their teachers. We believe that because of our status as professional sports figures and entertainers with national media exposure our personal participation in this program will greatly inspire and motivate these young people to maximize their talents and develop their untapped potential.

Your personal involvement will consist of visits to schools, churches, community centers, etc., to sign autographs and to speak to young people on the value of education: remaining drug-free, etc. These visits will be coordinated by the local Penny Campaign Coordinator. Please return the form below to indicate your willingness to assist our national efforts. Please provide me a telephone number so that we can contact you to plan your visits and appearances. The Penny Lover Coordinator for your area will contact you. I appreciate your personal involvement in this National Penny Campaign and support of our youth.

Yours truly,

Mel Blount, Chairman
National Penny Campaign

Please return to: ---------------------------------
Mel Blount, Chairman, National Penny Campaign
Penny Lovers of America, Inc.
P.O. Box 6141
Somerset, New Jersey 08875-6141

Dear Mel:

Yes, I will be happy to support the National Penny Campaign. I am enclosing $3.65 for my first year's pledge and commitment.

I can be contacted directly at telephone number:_____

Name_____

Address_____

City_____ State_____Zip_____

Tel. No.: Area Code (___)_____

[ ] I elect to pay my five (5) year commitment of $18.25 now. I will continue to save at least "one penny each day" for the Economic Emancipation Programs.

[ ] Also Mel, please send me_____ copies of the book, The Economic Emancipation of African-Americans, by Richard E. Barber, at $7.95 per copy plus $2.00 postage and handling. The amount of $_____is enclosed.

PENNY POWER • PENNY POWER • PENNY POWER

Certificate No._____

CERTIFICATE OF COMMITMENT
The Economic Emancipation of African-Americans

"Where there is no vision, the people perish."
Proverbs 29:18
"Thank God For the Vision"!!
R.E.B.

1. _____ pledge to support the goals and objectives of the Economic Emancipation Plan for a minimum period of five (5) years by saving at least one (1) penny each day for this historic national "self-help" economic development effort.

[ ] I am enclosing $3.65 for my first year's pledge and commitment. Future pledges of $3.65 annually are due on January 15th (Dr. Martin Luther King Jr.'s Birthday).

[ ] I elect to pay my five (5) year commitment of $18.25 now. I will continue to save at least "one penny each day" for the Economic Emancipation Programs.

Signed_____

Address_____

City_____ State_____Zip_____

Tel. No.: Area Code (   )_____

Return to:
  Mel Blount, Chairman, National Penny
  Campaign
  Penny Lovers of America, Inc.
  P.O. Box 6141
  Somerset, New Jersey 08875-6141

PENNY POWER • PENNY POWER • PENNY POWER

Dear Pastors and Church Leaders:

As professional athletes and entertainers, we have a very profound and serious obligation to provide a positive influence to millions of young people who idolize us as hero figures. In this regard, we are turning to the church community to form an alliance and partnership in order to meet this challenge and responsibility to our young people. As professional athletes and entertainers, we can get their attention and serve as positive role models. However, we fully realize that any worthwhile program to serve our young people should be based on Christian principles and values in order to enhance their spiritual growth as well as their physical, educational and emotional growth. For this reason, scores of professional athletes and entertainers have committed their time and resources in order to support the National Penny Campaign sponsored by the Penny Lovers of America, Inc., a non-profit organization based in Somerset, New Jersey. Our primary goal is to support the overall implementation of the

<u>Economic Emancipation Plan for African-Americans</u> which was developed by Richard E. Barber, Founder and National President of Penny Lovers of America, Inc.

The primary purpose and mission of Penny Lovers of America, Inc. is to convey a message of <u>Character-Building</u>, <u>Scholarship</u>, and <u>Patriotism</u> to the young people of America, ages 6-16. I have been elected to the Board of Directors of Penny Lovers of America and serve as Chairman of the National Penny Campaign.

Our national goal is to raise 1,000,000 pounds of pennies ($1,640,000.00) annually or 151.5 miles of pennies for scholarships and selected community projects, and to encourage participants to save "one penny each day" for the Penny Lovers organization on an on-going basis. The attached monologue entitled <u>A Penny Speaks</u>, by a penny itself provides our primary reasons for this National Penny Campaign.

Our second goal is to encourage at least 100,000 young people each year to commit to the principles of the <u>Power of Knowledge Pledge</u> (see attached) and sign it along with a parent/or guardian, and one of their teachers. We believe that because of our status as professional sports figures and entertainers with national media exposure our personal participation in this program will greatly inspire and motivate these young people to maximize their talents and develop their untapped potential.

We need your help in achieving these worthwhile goals. We are requesting that each church assist our efforts by participating as follows:

(1) Request that each church appoint a Penny Coordinator and raise from 10,000 to 20,000 pennies ($100.00 to $200.00, or 49 to 98 feet of pennies, or 61.3 to 122.6 pounds of pennies) annually by encouraging your members to bring in their pennies for this national effort.

(2) Make copies of "A Penny Speaks" available to your congregation or publish in the church bulletins.

(3) Make copies of the Power of Knowledge Pledge available to the young people in your congregation and encourage them to commit to its principles and sign it, along with a parent or guardian and one of their teachers. As the athletes tour the country raising pennies we intend

to autograph the <u>Power of Knowledge Pledge</u> for the young people once they are properly signed by the persons mentioned above. We want to encourage and motivate our young people to stay in school and develop their talent and untapped potential. We want to do that in the spirit of the motto of Penny Lovers of America, <u>Character-Building</u>, <u>Scholarship</u>, and <u>Patriotism</u>.

(4) After you have collected the pennies, send a check equivalent to the pennies collected to Penny Lovers of America, Inc.

(5) Please encourage members of your congregation to save at least "one penny each day" on an on-going basis for our efforts. Small banks will be made available to your congregation at a later date.

(6) Please complete and return the attached form to our National Headquarters indicating your church participation in this National Penny Campaign and our joint efforts to develop young people with a sense of responsibility and

personal values based on Christian principles.

We believe that this partnership--Pastors and Professional Athletes/Entertainers--you from the pulpit and professional athletes/entertainers from the sports arenas, theatres and concert halls--will have a very positive impact on our young people. We believe that such a partnership can provide new visions, new hope, and higher aspirations and achievements by our young people.

We look forward to working with you and hope that some of the athletes and entertainers can visit your congregation some time in the future.

Yours truly,

Mel Blount

Mel Blount
Former Pittsburgh Steeler and Chairman of the National Penny Campaign

Note: Please photocopy the form on the next page and return it to me.

THE ANNUAL PENNY CAMPAIGN

"WHERE THERE IS NO VISION, THE PEOPLE PERISH."
Proverbs 29:18

Return to:

Mel Blount, Chairman, National Penny Campaign
Penny Lovers of America, Inc.
P.O. Box 6141
Somerset, New Jersey 08875-6141

Dear Mel:

Our church will participate in the National Penny Campaign and become partners with you and your fellow athletes and entertainers in conveying a message of Character-Building, Scholarship, and Patriotism to our young people.

Name of Church _____

Pastor _____

Address _____

City _____, State _____ Zip ____

Tel. No.: Area Code (_____) _____

Penny Coordinator _____

Our goal and commitment is to raise [____] $100.00 (49 feet of pennies, or 61.3 pounds of pennies), or [____] $200.00 (98 feet of pennies, or 122.6 pounds of pennies) annually for the Economic Emancipation Programs.

[ ] We are enclosing our first year's commitment of $_____, or ____ feet of pennies, or _____ pounds of pennies.

[ ] Also Mel, please send me _____ copies of the book The Economic Emancipation Of African-Americans, by Richard E. Barber, at 7.95 per copy plus $2.00 for postage and handling. The amount of $_____ is enclosed.

PENNY POWER • PENNY POWER • PENNY POWER

APPENDIX VII

THE POWER OF KNOWLEDGE PLEDGE

I PLEDGE:

1.   I now realize that the greatest power in the world is the power of knowledge.

2.   I want to be smart. Dumb, misinformed people go through life missing so many rewards that could be theirs.

3.   I will learn my basic skills and be expert in them.

4.   I will read books on the subjects that interest me most. But I will also read books and articles on other subjects to broaden my awareness of what is happening in the world around me.

5.   I will discuss at dinner time what I have learned or questioned at school today.

6.   I will study the ideas and dreams of our history to see how they can help me today.

7.   I will set aside some time each day to think about my future, to discuss it with people I respect and to work on accumulating the knowledge that can guarantee that future.

8.   I further pledge to remain drug free by "just saying NO" to drugs and other substances which will defile and destroy my mind and body.

9.   I pledge this to those who love me and are trying to help me succeed. More importantly, I pledge it to myself.

_____

Student signature

_____

Teacher (I'll help you)

_____

Parent/Guardian (endorsed with great love)

PENNY POWER • PENNY POWER • PENNY POWER

Authorized adaptation of a message as published in the Wall Street Journal by United Technologies Corporation, Hartford, Connecticut 06101 in 1979.

APPENDIX VIII

SELECT LISTING OF AFRICAN-AMERICAN CONSUMER SPENDING

PRODUCT	BLACK SPENDING
Milk Flavoring	$ 65,690,900
Frozen Orange Juice	131,770,980
Powdered Fruit Flavored Drinks	22,235,500
Powdered Soft Drinks	94,936,160
Frozen Pizza	91,062,180
Corn/Tortilla Chips	9,718,599
Baby Food and Cereal	146,133,900
Baby Oil and Lotion	10,454,744
Baby Powder	10,785,347
Disposable Diapers	195,380,900
Pre-Moistened Cleansing Wipes	15,564,641
Children's Vitamins	144,554,000
Hot Breakfast Cereal	49,325,650
Decaffinated Instant & Freeze Dried Coffee	198,830,400
Orange Juice (bottles, cans or cartons)	106,480,000
Baked Beans	55,871,970
Spaghetti & Macaroni Products	53,895,457
Vegetables	149,248,440
Plastic Garbage Bags	10,125,060
Air Freshener Sprays & Room Deodorizers	16,871,910
Floor Wax & Polishers	26,298,800
Malt Liquor	232,126,400
Cola	1,427,834,800
Other Sodas	2,299,000,000
Chewing Gum	193,634,157
Hard Roll Candy	64,982,500
Cold, Allergy and Sinus Remedies	75,994,380
Cough Syrup	51,554,782
Laxatives	55,383,328
Nasal Sprays	15,488,000
Breath Fresheners	10,769,220
Deodorants and anti-perspirants	10,769,220
Bath Oil and Other Bath Additives	21,010,000
Records and Tape Cartridges (blanks)	441,840,000

Source: World Institute of Black Communications, Inc. Data based on index figures provided by Simmons Market Research Bureau.

APPENDIX IX

AFRICAN PROVERBS TO PONDER

1. The ruin of a nation begins in the homes of its people.

2. It is no shame at all to work for money.

3. When you are rich, you are hated; when you are poor, you are dispised.

4. Knowledge is better than riches.

5. Rain does not fall on one roof alone.

6. He who conceals his disease cannot expect to be cured.

7. A too modest man goes hungry.

8. She who does not yet know how to walk, cannot climb a ladder.

9. What one hopes for is always better than what one has.

10. The man on his feet carries off the share of the man sitting down.

11. To make preparations does not spoil the trip.

12. Knowledge is like a garden: If if is not cultivated, it cannot be harvested.

13. When a needle falls into a deep well, many people will look into the well, but few will be ready to go down after it.

14. Two flavors confuse the palate.

15. A white dog does not bite another white dog.

16. One finger alone cannot kill even a louse.

17. A man who continually laments is not heeded.

18. Talking with one another is loving one another.

19. Cross the river in a crowd and the crocodile won't eat you.

20. He who loves money must labor.

21. Before one cooks, one must have the meat.

22. Not all flowers of a tree produce fruit.

23. If you watch your pot, your food will not burn.

24. Two eyes see better than one.

25. The rat cannot call the cat to account.

26. He who is sick will not refuse medicine.

27. The day on which one starts out is not the time to start one's preparations.

28. He who is being carried does not realize how far the town is.

29. The stone in the water does not know how hot the hill is, parched by the sun.

30. Someone else's legs do you no good in traveling.

31. Fine words do not produce food.

32. When the mouse laughs at the cat, there is a hole nearby.

33. When one is in trouble, one remembers God.

34. Not to know is bad; not to wish to know is worse.

35. If the stomach-ache were in the foot, one would go lame.

36. Horns do not grow before the head.

37. If you are building a house and a nail breaks, do you stop building, or do you change the nail?

38. The opportunity that God sends does not wake up him who is asleep.

39. When you know who his friend is, you know who he is.

40. The truth is like gold: Keep it locked up and you will find it exactly as you first put it away.

41. A healthy ear can stand hearing sick words.

42. If a centipede loses a leg, it does not prevent him from walking.

43. If a little tree grows in the shade of a larger tree, it will die small.

44. An intelligent enemy is better than a stupid friend.

45. A cow must graze where she is tied.

46. To try and to fail, is not laziness.

47. He who does not shave you, does not cut you.

48. Do not tell the man who is carrying you that he stinks.

49. Poverty is slavery.

50. Copying everybody else all the time, the monkey one day cut his throat.

51. Even an ant may harm an elephant.

52. The horse who arrives early gets good drinking water.

53. A roaring lion kills no game.

54. We start as fools and become wise through experience.

55. Do not walk into a snake-pit with your eyes open.

56. Wisdom does not come overnight.

57. If you climb up a tree, you must climb down the same tree.

58. He who has goods can sell them.

59. He who does not mend his clothes will soon not have none.

60. Let your love be like misty rain, coming softly, but flooding the river.

May the wisdom conveyed in these African Proverbs transform our minds, and give us thoughtful insights for positive strategy development, and a larger vision which will manifest itself in our daily lives on our journey toward Economic Emancipation.

Richard E. Barber, Sr.

Note:

The above <u>African Proverbs To Ponder</u> were compiled by Charlotte and Wolf Leslau in the book AFRICAN PROVERBS, Peter Pauper Press, Inc.

A Special Tribute To My Father

My father, the late John Barber, would often encourage my three brothers (Fletcher, John Haywood and Elbert) and me, and five sisters (Luverna, Lila Mae, Lillian Arlene, Loretta and Linda) with one of his favorite sayings when we were facing difficult and challenging situations growing up on the farm. He would say to us:

"Children, the darkest hour of the night is just before daybreak."

Thank you "Papa" for your wisdom and caring.

APPENDIX X

DR. ROBERT SCHULLER'S QUOTATIONS

Beginning is half done!

Do what you can, where you are with what you have.

When your knees knock, kneel on them.

The difficult we do immediately, the impossible takes a little longer.

The "Is" must never catch up with the "ought."

Building boys is better than mending men.

Great people are just ordinary people with an extra ordinary amount of determination.

God's delays are not God's denials.

A man's life consists not of what he has, but what he is.

Wrinkles should merely show where the smiles have been.

Imagine being in this glorious world with grateful hearts and no one to thank.

A star is best seen a night.

Your future is your friend.

When you fail to plan, you plan to fail.

Let go, let God take over.

Yes, Lord! There is no gain without pain.

Change your thoughts and you can change the world.

I'd rather attempt to do something great and fail, than attempt to do nothing and succeed.

You are God's project and God never fails.

Inch by inch anything's a cinch.

Problems are guideposts, not stop signs.

Do it now!

Gifts given to God are seeds planted in fertile ground.

Love is my deciding to make your problem my problem.

Begin where you are.

Bloom where you are planted.

God don't sponsor no flops.

Hallelujah--Anyway.

Count the apples in the seed.

Attempt great things for God - expect great things from God.

Connect with God-Power - Now.

Turn your scars into stars.

Wherever I am, God Is.

Trying times are time to triumph (Try + Umph)

What you are is God's gift to you. What you make of yourself is your gift to God.

Nothing is too great for God's power. Nothing is too small for God's love.

To Succeed you need to solve only two problems:
1) Get started, 2) Never Quit.

God loves every person but God isn't satisfied with any person.

He has a better plan for your life.

Better to do something imperfectly than to do nothing perfectly.

The secret of happiness is so simple - find a hurt and heal it.

Build a dream and the dream will build you.

Today respond to that beautiful idea! No waste is so tragic as the waste of a good idea.

Great people are only common people who have committed themselves with enthusiasm to outstanding goals.

Failure doesn't mean that God has abandoned you, it does mean God has a better idea.

To solve your problem, simply think bigger - or think longer - than you ever have before.

Let your worry drain out and let God's peace flow in.

People who never change their minds are either perfect to begin with - or stubborn forever after.

There are infinite possibilities in little beginnings if God is in it.

Life is a collection of results of choices you have made.

I am a child of God and that's somebody!

I will make my plans big enough for God to fit in them.

I have to believe it, before I'll see it.

Dreams come true when I tap into God's power.

I will focus my thoughts on God, not on my problem.

God loves me anyway.

God will help me to keep on...keeping on.

Success ideas will only work if I do.

God is stronger and bigger than my problem.

Failure doesn't mean that God has abandoned me...It does mean that God has a better idea.

My shadows never stand still.

I will plan my tomorrow for I have to live there.

The difficult we do immediately - the impossible takes a little longer.

When your knees knock kneel on them.

Turn your scars into stars.

The "Is" must never catch up with the "ought."

Inch by inch, anything is a cinch.

Problems are guidelines, not stop signs.

God's delays are not God's denials.

Wrinkles should show where smiles have been.

Success is never certain, and failure is never final.

What you give is what you get.

It takes two to make a miracle.

When you fail to plan, you plan to fail.

God does His biggest projects through His littlest people.

Quitters never win and winners never quit.

Make your decisions on "Godsability" not your ability.

Look at what you have left, not at what you have lost.

I am God's project and God never fails.

Whatever your mind can achieve, you can achieve.

Nobody has any business feeling unneeded in a world where there is so much hurt.

Build a dream and the dream will build you.

Attempt impossibilities for God, expect possibilities from God.

Today's impossibilities are tomorrow's miracles.

An impossibility is the gateway to progress.

This year's success was last year's impossibility.

An impossibility is a big idea that calls for bigger thinking.

Don't let impossibilities intimidate you, do let impossibilities motivate you.

Tackle an impossibility and start living by faith.

Reach the peak of possibilities, and catch a peek of new impossibilities.

Every problem is a possibility in disguise.

Problems start to shrink: when you start to think: It's possible.

It's possible: to face the music with God's song in your heart.

It's possible: to make headway if you'll face the headwinds

It's possible: if you build on your hopes - not on your hurts.

INDEX